ASIAN AFTER WORK

ADAM LIAW

Simple food for every day

hachette
AUSTRALIA

For my mum, who always cooked for me after work.

CONTENTS

INTRODUCTION   6
EASY MENUS   14

SUNDAY   18

White Chicken Stock   20
Garlic & Shallot Oil   21
Liaw Family XO Sauce   22
Hot Chilli Oil (Ra-Yu)   24
Fish Sauce Ponzu   25
Faster Master   28
Umami Sauce   29
Pickled Carrot & Daikon (Do Chua)   30
Light Teriyaki   32
Chilli Furikake   33
Balinese Roast Pork Belly with Fresh Sambal   36
Chicken Adobo   39
Two-To-One Rice   40
Lions' Heads   43
Northern Chinese Roast Lamb   44
Pi-Pa Roast Duck   49
Leche Flan   50
Asami's Cheesecake   53

MONDAY   54

Soy-Dressed Tofu   57
Bang-Bang Chicken Salad   58
XO Beef & Broccoli   61
Hot-Buttered Onigiri   62
Short Soup   65
Savoury Egg Custard   66
Tempura Pumpkin & Onion with Curry Salt   70
Singapore Noodles   73
Miso-Roasted Eggplant   74
Asazuke   77
Spinach & Sesame Salad   78
Master Stock Poached Chicken Breast   81
Vietnamese Affogato   82

TUESDAY   84

XO Prawns & Snow Peas   87
'No. 88' Special Fried Rice   88
Hailam Noodles   91
Teriyaki Chicken   92
Crispy Squid with Chilli Furikake   95
Mille-Feuille with Chilli Ponzu   96
Prawn & Avocado Doria   101
Salt & Pepper Pork Belly   102
Cheat's Claypot   107
Korean Pork & Kimchi Casserole (Kimchi Chigae)   108
Japanese Tofu Salad   111
Spicy Beansprout Salad   112
Chicken with Garlic & Crispy Lime Leaves   115
Lychee & Coconut Granita   116

WEDNESDAY 118

Japanese Triple-Fried Chicken (Kara Age)	121
Dry Wonton Noodles	122
Beef Bowls (Gyudon)	125
Fish Sauce Roast Chicken	126
Brown Rice Congee with Crab	129
Sang Choy Bao	130
Crying Tiger	133
Caramelised Lemongrass Pork Chops	134
Crystal Prawns with Celery	137
Fresh Herb & Prawn Salad	138
Chicken Fat Noodles	141
Salmon & Avocado Donburi	142
Malaysian Deep-Fried Bananas (Goreng Pisang)	145
Simplest Coconut Ice Cream	146

THURSDAY 148

Kachumber	150
Winter Pork & Miso Soup (Tonjiru)	153
Fillet Steak with Red Miso Butter	154
Pak Choy with Oyster Sauce	157
Chicken Kra-Pow	158
Master Stock Fried Chicken & Five-Spice Salt	161
Mushroom Rice	162
Nagoya-Style Chicken Wings	165
Beef Bulgogi	166
Japanese Beef Curry	169
Beef Korokke with Miso-Mustard Mayonnaise	170
BBQ Genghis Khan	173
Sesame & Honey Ice Cream	174

FRIDAY 176

Bibimbap	178
Seafood Pajeon	181
Duck Buns	182
Ginger-Fried Pork	185
Malaysian Barbecue Fish	186
Kinilaw	189
Penang Achar	192
Ocean Trout with Garlic & Soy	195
Grilled Prawns with Salty Lime	196
Sweet & Sour Pork	199
Pineapple Fried Rice	200
Yum Cha Mango Pancakes	203
Sweet Almond Pudding with Poached Apricots	204

SATURDAY 206

Pan Sushi	209
Dry-Baked Lamb Chop Curry with Sweet Potato	210
Sugarcane Prawn Rolls	213
Pork & Prawn Wontons	214
Duck Shoyu Ramen	219
Vietnamese Beef Stew (Bo Kho)	222
Crab & Lettuce Fried Rice	225
Black Pepper Beef	226
Dragon Wings	229
Siu Mai	231
Coconut & Tamarind Pork Belly	234
Hwachae	237
Chocolate & Berry Honey Toast	238

GLOSSARY	244
INDEX	246

INTRODUCTION

Creating authentic Asian cuisine has never been the exclusive domain of the chef. Traditionally it has been driven by working families – dishes that are decades and centuries old have persisted because they are being cooked again and again, in ordinary homes around Asia, by people like you and me.

I worked as a lawyer for more than a decade, and I know intimately the burden of finishing a long and exhausting day at the office, only to head home to an empty kitchen. At those times it's easy to turn to takeaway foods, convenience foods and, in our darkest moments, cereal straight from the box as we watch the late news. But the idea of wanting to cook and eat the food we love with limited time isn't a creation of modern society. The generations of cooks who came before us, and who built Asian cuisines through thousands of repetitions, were not chefs in the sole pursuit of gastronomic excellence; they were hard-working people with worries and sore backs, to whom a hot meal to end a day's labour was more a privilege than a promise.

It seems quite unbelievable that, even with all our modern conveniences, appliances and supermarkets, we are now less able to make real food than someone who was doing it a century ago on a wood fire, with no refrigerator, after a day's manual labour, and all after growing their own vegetables for the pot.

But this is not a call to turn back the clock. It's an appeal to think differently about how we want to cook and eat. The idea of simple food does not need to be a salad thrown together in haste, dressed from a bottle and eaten as we rush from one distraction to the next. Nor does it need to be a soulless shadow of a dish that has had all the joy sucked out of it in the name of speed.

As a child, I remember watching my mother beginning dinner preparations in the morning before going to work – an investment of her time that would be returned when she came home at night to eight hungry kids and two adults to feed. That would be a daunting task for anyone, but she never failed to have our dinner on the table in moments, a daily gift repaid with full bellies and wide smiles.

Today when I visit my elderly grandmother, almost even before a hello she'll ask me whether I've eaten, and reel off a host of dishes she could make for me from ingredients she has in her fridge or pantry – dishes that would be ready in just a few minutes. The idea of creating food that is affordable, fast and flavourful is where Asian cuisines have excelled for centuries.

Instead of looking for corners to cut, or shortcuts to take, and consequently losing our way with food, we can choose dishes that suit our lifestyles, that reflect not just how we want to eat but also how we want to cook. This book is full of those dishes; the kinds of dishes I make after coming home from a day of work, and that I find a pleasure to cook, rather than a chore.

I CAN'T COOK

One of the charming truths about cooking is that anyone can do it. It doesn't take superhuman strength or unique talent to put something in a pan and take it out again, or to follow a set of instructions in a recipe. When it comes to the basic mechanics of cooking, most cooks – good and bad – have the same two hands, two eyes, a nose and a mouth, and that's all you really need.

Learning to cook has been the most important and rewarding thing I have done in my life. There can be no easier way to make people happy, and no investment of your time better made than in ensuring you will eat well, and that your family will eat well, for as long as you are able to stand at a stove.

Confidence and skill in the kitchen, as in many things, comes with practice. If you say you can't even fry an egg, try frying five eggs in a row and don't worry about the ones that fail. I promise you that before you are finished the fifth, you will have learned how it is done. Twenty minutes and five eggs is a small price to pay for a skill you will have for the rest of your life.

I DON'T KNOW WHAT TO HAVE FOR DINNER

Most families have no more than a handful of dishes on their menu – trusty favourites they cook with regularity. There's nothing wrong with cooking what you like, but getting stuck in a culinary rut is a common pitfall. It can make spending time in the kitchen seem like more work to be done, and even eating can become more of an inevitability than a pleasure.

If you were to write down all the dishes you comfortably and regularly cook for dinner – and I mean *actually* cook, and do so on a regular basis, not those you cooked once and promptly abandoned – how many would there be? Perhaps five? Ten? Regardless of the number in your repertoire, it's actually more interesting to consider

how these dishes are made. They probably contain no more than ten ingredients, use simple processes such as braising, frying, roasting or steaming, and require less than half an hour of your time at a bench or over a stove. These are the parameters many people set for themselves, and even if you choose to stay within them, you might find them more spacious than you thought.

I have selected the recipes in this book for the most part to suit the way people really cook – simple dishes using simple processes. From Monday to Friday there are easy weekday meals, and on Saturday and Sunday there are some recipes and ideas for cooking ahead that might make your mid-week meals even simpler.

As you look through the dishes in this book, think about how they might make their way into your own family menu. Just adding one or two to your repertoire can make a world of difference to your enjoyment of everyday meals.

I DON'T HAVE TIME TO COOK

It can sure feel like that when you are tired at the end of a day, but it is possible to put together a proper dinner. Even for the truly hurried, it is a simple and convenient fact that there is very little correlation between how long a dish takes to cook, how complicated it is, and how good it tastes.

A **Lychee & Coconut Granita** (page 116), for example, can be made by blending just two or three ingredients for twenty seconds then putting them in the freezer. A homemade plate of **Chicken Kra-Pow** (page 158) involves no more than five minutes in front of a stove, but one taste might lead you to throw away your takeaway menus.

When we think of cooking, we often think of bubbling pots, clattering frypans and open flames, but the lion's share of cooking is in preparation. Imagine how long we would wait in a restaurant if the floor staff took your order and only then did the kitchen start cutting up the vegetables and making the stocks. Yet this is the task so many set themselves each night when dinner starts with a bag of groceries arriving at a kitchen bench and ends with a pile of dirty plates in the sink.

If we separate our time in the kitchen into preparation, cooking, serving and cleaning, these discrete tasks make creating a meal all the more manageable. Even something as simple as cleaning cutting boards, mixing bowls and knives after prep and before cooking leaves an empty sink – so that after the meal, dishes can be simply rinsed and put into the dishwasher (or into the hands of a child similarly tasked), then it's all done.

Another advantage of separating prep and cooking is that it makes the cooking part easier. Rather than racing against an overheating pot to frantically slice a forgotten ingredient, if you have prepared and put everything in its rightful place, you can focus on the cooking. Without stress or hurry, the process of making the evening meal then becomes something to look forward to, rather than something to dread.

Once separated from cooking, preparation can also be done well in advance, instead of shoe-horned into those precious few hours between the end of work and the start of sleep. Ten minutes on Sunday afternoon to make a batch of **Light Teriyaki** (page 32) could lead to an effortless **Teriyaki Chicken** (page 92) on Tuesday, **Nagoya-Style Chicken Wings** (page 165) on Thursday, or a warm bowl of **Duck Shoyu Ramen** (page 219) on Saturday.

A jar of homemade **Liaw Family XO Sauce** (page 22) may take an hour of relaxed preparation at an otherwise idle time on the weekend, but once you have it in the fridge, you have months' worth of **XO Prawns & Snow Peas** (page 87), **Crab & Lettuce Fried Rice** (page 225) or **XO Beef & Broccoli** (page 61) to look forward to. These are dishes that can be ready in just minutes and that you will have made with your own hands.

Prep when you have time, and cook only when you need to.

I DON'T KNOW ANYTHING ABOUT ASIAN FOOD

If you haven't grown up around Asian cuisines, they can seem a bit of a mystery, with unpronounceable names, strange ingredients and exotic flavours. But what once seemed exotic is now a common part of what we eat in Australia, and our desire for variety and quality in Asian food is unsurpassed in the Western world. Australians today have little trouble telling their teriyaki from their tempura, or their bulgogi from their bibimbap. However, as popular as it is in Australia, Asian food is still most frequently eaten at restaurants and out of takeaway containers, rather than cooked in our own kitchens.

It's not hard to see why people can be intimidated by the thought of cooking Asian cuisines. A peek into the kitchen of most Asian restaurants reveals whirling woks and leaping flames, a world apart from the calm and ordered kitchens many of us like to have at home. Asian grocers fill to bursting with thousands of bottles, jars and cans full of unknowable sauces and pastes, the colourful labels meaning well but ultimately providing no guidance whatsoever. Even menus in Asian restaurants can stretch a mile long, with mangled and inscrutable translations of mysterious dishes. If a restaurant can't even translate it on a menu, what hope do we all have in our own kitchens?

But no matter from which languages these dishes speak, the one thing common to every tongue is its ability to taste. If you can eat Asian food you can cook it. There is no undefined magic nor secret handshake behind it. Asian cuisines strive to draw the best natural flavours from just a few ingredients, judiciously chosen and treated simply.

If you just throw a handful of 'mixed vegetables' into a 'stir-fry' and smother it in thick sauce, the taste of your dish will be defined only by the sauce and not by the vegetables themselves. Instead, choose your vegetables for their flavour rather than their food group. A dish of **Crystal Prawns with Celery** (page 137) should taste of celery, and should taste completely different with spring onion substituted in its place. Your **Black Pepper Beef** (page 226) should change its characteristics if you choose baby corn over green capsicum.

When sourcing ingredients, you can approach these recipes confident that they won't be sending you into uncharted territory. In this book I've deliberately chosen ingredients that are common, available and versatile; the kinds of ingredients that can be used for multiple dishes, rather than bought for a single use, cluttering a pantry shelf for a lifetime. Most can be found in any ordinary Australian supermarket. Take a closer look at the Asian food section where you shop: you may be surprised by what you find. One or two special ingredients in these recipes might require a trip to your nearest Asian grocer, but look at that as an adventure rather than an imposition.

Every kitchen has its own collection of measuring implements. Throughout this book measurements vary between cups and metric to suit each recipe and make the method as clear and simple to follow as possible. A basic conversion would be: one cup equals 250ml, one tablespoon equals 20ml and one teaspoon equals 5ml.

There is no reason to be intimidated by Asian cooking. You are already armed with everything you need to tackle the recipes in this book. If you can roll a meatball, you can cook **Lions' Heads** (page 43). If you can roast a chicken, you can make **Pi-Pa Roast Duck** (page 49). If you can grill a steak and stir a bowl, you can conquer the **Crying Tiger** (page 133).

I hope these ideas and recipes equip you to change your evening meals for the better, and that they bring you as much pleasure as they have for me. Every dish you cook from this book is another step towards a fascinating world of simple and appealing Asian cookery.

Enjoy the adventure.

EASY MENUS

The dishes in this book mostly stand alone as meals in themselves, but they can also be combined into dinners for sharing the Asian way. Four main dishes and a dessert should be plenty for six to eight guests, but if you have more guests coming, add another dish or two and bump up the quantities.

THE OLD FAITHFUL

SERVES 6–12

It's always nice having a go-to menu to rely on for a dinner party, and one that can be scaled up or down depending on how many people you've invited. This menu is a mix of easy dishes that can be prepared in advance and others you can finish off just before serving.

Fresh Herb & Prawn Salad	138
Duck Buns	182
Soy-Dressed Tofu	57
Chicken with Garlic & Crispy Lime Leaves	115
Ocean Trout with Garlic & Soy	195
Coconut & Tamarind Pork Belly	234
Two-To-One Rice	40
Sweet Almond Pudding with Poached Apricots	204

THAI STREETS

SERVES 6

You don't need a plane ticket to Bangkok or a takeaway menu to enjoy a delicious Thai feast.

Fresh Herb & Prawn Salad	138
Chicken Kra-Pow or	158
Fish Sauce Roast Chicken	126
Salt & Pepper Pork Belly	102
Pineapple Fried Rice	200
Simplest Coconut Ice Cream	146

GOOD EVENING, VIETNAM

SERVES 6–8

The fresh flavours of Vietnamese food are perfect for a summer's evening dinner party. Serve with rice.

Sugarcane Prawn Rolls	213
Pickled Carrot & Daikon (Do Chua)	30
Fresh Herb & Prawn Salad	138
Caramelised Lemongrass Pork Chops	134
Vietnamese Beef Stew (Bo Kho)	222
Vietnamese Affogato	82

AT–HOME IZAKAYA

SERVES 6

Nights out at casual Japanese restaurants with great food and good company are among my fondest memories of living in Japan. Serve with lots of ice-cold beer and perhaps a sneaky sake or two.

Japanese Triple-Fried Chicken (Kara Age)	121
Spinach & Sesame Salad	78
Japanese Tofu Salad	111
Ginger-Fried Pork	185
Beef Korokke with Miso-Mustard Mayonnaise	170
Asazuke	77
Sesame & Honey Ice Cream	174

SEOUL FOOD

SERVES 4–6

This Korean menu keeps things authentic and simple. You can vary the quantities of the bulgogi depending on how many mouths you need to feed.

Seafood Pajeon	181
Spicy Beansprout Salad	112
Beef Bulgogi	166
Hwachae	237

'NIKU-NASHI' JAPANESE VEGETARIAN
SERVES 6

Stepping away from our carnivorous side for a while can be a good thing, and in this vegetarian Japanese menu you can do so without feeling like you're missing anything.

Miso-Roasted Eggplant	74
Japanese Tofu Salad	111
Tempura Pumpkin & Onion with Curry Salt	70
Asazuke	77
Mushroom Rice *or*	162
Hot-Buttered Onigiri	62
Asami's Cheesecake	53

PHOENIX BANQUET
SERVES 8

This Chinese banquet is both simple to cook and impressive to serve. While in a restaurant this would come one course at a time, for home just put all the savoury dishes on the table at the same time and dive in.

Siu Mai	231
Crystal Prawns with Celery	137
XO Beef & Broccoli	61
Pi-Pa Roast Duck	49
Pak Choy with Oyster Sauce	157
Crab & Lettuce Fried Rice	225
Sweet Almond Pudding with Poached Apricots	204

BUDDHA GETS ON THE TREADMILL
SERVES 6

This menu of healthy Asian dishes would be perfect for a mid-week dinner party. There's no more than a few minutes' preparation in each dish, but once on the table it is an impressive and healthy spread.

Japanese Tofu Salad	111
Spinach & Sesame Salad	78
Grilled Prawns with Salty Lime	196
Crying Tiger	133
Lychee & Coconut Granita	116

THE GRILL
SERVES 8–10

This menu puts an Asian spin on a Sunday barbecue. A few salads, a bit of seafood and some marinated meats on a hot grill is a great afternoon with friends in anyone's language.

Penang Achar	192
Spinach & Sesame Salad	78
Fresh Herb & Prawn Salad	138
Grilled Prawns with Salty Lime	196
Malaysian Barbecue Fish	186
Caramelised Lemongrass Pork Chops	134
BBQ Genghis Khan	173
Leche Flan	50

THE GREAT WALL (10% OFF FOR TAKEAWAY)
SERVES 8

These dishes take me back to a childhood of suburban Chinese restaurants, when dishes came on sizzling hotplates and we gasped in awe at desserts with sparklers stuck in them.

Sang Choy Bao	130
Short Soup	65
Sweet & Sour Pork	199
XO Prawns & Snow Peas	87
Black Pepper Beef	226
'No.88' Special Fried Rice	88
Yum Cha Mango Pancakes	203

FINGER FEASTS
SERVES 10–100

If you have a big group to feed, finger food is definitely the way to go. These dishes can be produced in huge quantities to satisfy the hungry crowds.

Pan Sushi	209
Pork & Prawn Wontons	214
Crispy Squid with Chilli Furikake	95
Nagoya-Style Chicken Wings	165
Dragon Wings	229
Duck Buns	182
Asami's Cheesecake	53

SUNDAY

This basic unsalted chicken stock cooks low and slow, leaving a perfectly clear stock suitable for almost any purpose for which you may otherwise use water - a base for adding flavour to casseroles and soups or cooking rice and vegetables. The stock will keep in the fridge for a week and you can also freeze it in small batches to use when you need.

WHITE CHICKEN STOCK

MAKES: 2½ LITRES
PREP: 5 MINUTES / **COOK:** 4–6 HOURS

Carcass and bones from 1 whole deboned chicken,
    or 500g chicken bones
2½ litres water

Place the carcass and bones in a large saucepan or stock pot, cover with water and bring to a rapid boil. Discard all the liquid, remove the carcass and bones and rinse them under cold water to remove any scum. Wash the pot to remove any scum sticking to the sides.

Return the carcass and bones to the pot, cover with 2½ litres of water and place over very low heat, partially covered, for 4–6 hours. The liquid should be steaming and any bubbles rising to the surface should be few and very small. Do not let it come to the boil.

Discard the solids and strain the stock through a fine sieve. Refrigerate and skim off any solid fat after it is chilled.

TIP

Keep any fat you skim off after refrigerating the stock for frying rice or Chicken Fat Noodles (page 141). If you want a stronger stock, use more bones.

An infused oil can be used to add flavour to stir-fries, blanched vegetables, salad dressings or anything, really, but remember that you will need to add salt to season. This one is perfect in a dressing for noodle dishes such as Dry Wonton Noodles (page 122).

GARLIC & SHALLOT OIL

MAKES: ABOUT 500 MILLILITRES
PREP: 10 MINUTES / **COOK:** 1 HOUR

500ml peanut oil, or other vegetable oil
150g red or golden shallots (about 5 large shallots),
    peeled and chopped
80g garlic (about 12 cloves), peeled and
    roughly chopped

Heat the oven to 100°C. Heat a few tablespoons of the oil in a small ovenproof saucepan and add the shallots and garlic. Toss over medium heat for a few minutes until softened and just starting to brown. Add the remaining oil and continue to heat until it starts to bubble vigorously.

Remove from the heat and transfer to the oven for 1 hour. Allow to cool, then strain off the solids. Store the flavoured oil in the fridge for up to 6 months.

TIP
Use the solids strained from this oil to add flavour to casseroles and stir-fries.

LIAW FAMILY XO SAUCE

XO sauce is a relative newcomer to Cantonese cuisine, appearing only in the 1980s. Named after XO Cognac – the height of sophistication in Hong Kong at the time – there are thousands of versions around. The fact that it is found all over the world is testament to the constant progression and invention in Asian cuisines (and in all cuisines). Don't be afraid to make changes to the recipe to make it your own. This is one recipe you can hand down for generations. Start a tradition.

MAKES: 2½ CUPS
PREP: 30 MINUTES / **WAIT:** 1 HOUR / **COOK:** 40 MINUTES

50g dried scallops
50g dried shrimp
2 cups peanut oil
4 large red or golden shallots, peeled and finely chopped
6 large red chillies, deseeded and finely chopped
6 large cloves garlic, peeled and finely chopped
50g prosciutto, sliced as finely as possible
1 tsp salt
1 tsp caster sugar
3 tsp chilli powder (preferably Korean)
1 tbsp dark soy sauce

Soak the scallops and shrimp separately, each in 1 cup of hot water for at least 1 hour. Drain well (reserve the strained liquid – see Tip below) and shred the scallops by rubbing them between your fingers. Roughly grind the drained shrimp in a mortar and pestle or food processor.

Heat 1 cup of the peanut oil in a wok or large saucepan over a medium heat and fry the shallots, chilli and garlic for 10 minutes, or until fragrant and the oil separates from the solids. Add the shredded scallops, ground shrimp, prosciutto, salt, sugar, chilli powder and soy sauce, stir well and fry for a further 10 minutes.

Add the remaining oil, reduce the heat to very low and simmer for 20 minutes, or until the XO sauce is oily and jammy. Allow to cool and transfer to a sterilised jar. The XO sauce will keep in the fridge for months.

TIP
The dried scallops in this recipe are a little expensive, but they're a necessary addition, and the versatility of this magnificent sauce makes it worth a special trip to an Asian grocery to get them. The reserved soaking liquid from the scallops and shrimp can be added to stocks, soups, stir-fries, or to the water used to cook rice or congee (Brown Rice Congee with Crab, page 129).

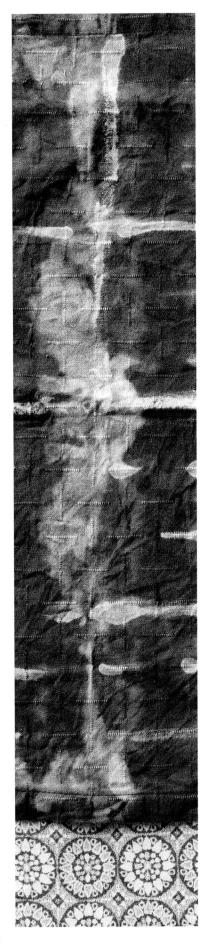

Ra-yu, or hot chilli oil, is a great addition to dipping sauces for dumplings. Use it in soups and dressings, and even for pan- or stir-frying seafood. Korean chilli powder has larger flakes than other chilli powders and gives the oil a deeper red colour.

HOT CHILLI OIL (RA-YU)

MAKES: 500 MILLILITRES
PREP: 5 MINUTES / **COOK:** 1 HOUR

500ml peanut oil, or other vegetable oil
½ brown onion, peeled and roughly chopped
3 cloves garlic, peeled and roughly chopped
3 tsp Korean chilli powder, or 3 tbsp dried chilli flakes

Heat the oven to 100°C. Heat a few tablespoons of the oil in a small ovenproof saucepan and add the onion and garlic. Toss over medium heat for a few minutes until softened and just starting to brown. Add the remaining oil and continue to heat for 1–2 minutes.

Stir through the chilli powder, remove from the heat and transfer to the oven for 1 hour. Turn off the oven and allow the oil to cool inside it. Strain off the solids and store the chilli oil in the fridge. It will keep for up to 12 months.

TIP
For a more decadent and flavourful prawn or lobster chilli oil, add some raw prawn or lobster shells together with the onion and garlic and fry in the saucepan until they turn red.

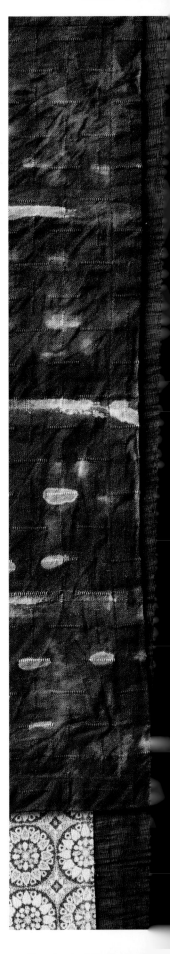

Ponzu is a basic Japanese sauce used for everything from steamed meat and fish to salad dressings. A more traditional ponzu adds flavour through bonito flakes and kombu seaweed, but this simpler version packs a punch of umami with the addition of fish sauce.

FISH SAUCE PONZU

MAKES: 375 MILLILITRES
PREP: 5 MINUTES / **COOK:** 5 MINUTES / **STAND:** 1 HOUR

75ml sake
75ml mirin
¼ tsp caster sugar
150ml light soy sauce
1 tsp fish sauce
Juice of 1 large lemon (about 75ml)

Bring the sake, mirin and sugar to the boil in a small saucepan and simmer for 1 minute. Add the soy sauce and fish sauce and return to the boil.

Remove from the heat and stir through the lemon juice. Allow to stand for 1 hour, strain to remove any lemon pulp or seeds, transfer to a container and chill in the fridge until ready to use. It will keep in the fridge for up to a month.

TIP

For a traditional ponzu, leave out the fish sauce and add 3g bonito flakes and a 10 × 10cm square of kombu seaweed together with the lemon juice.

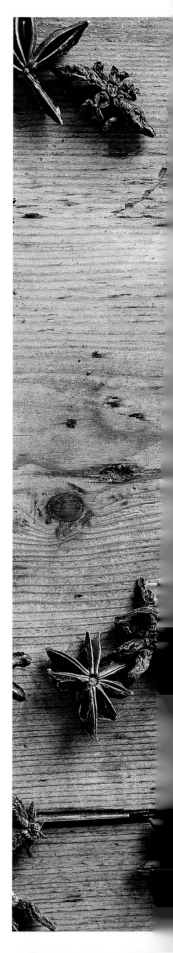

A master stock is an excellent, all-purpose liquid for poaching, braising or even using as a sauce for stir-frying. This quick and simple version uses just a few ingredients to create something that's always in the freezer, ready and waiting to add a lot of flavour with very little effort.

FASTER MASTER

MAKES: 2 LITRES
PREP: 5 MINUTES / **COOK:** 30 MINUTES

1½ litres White Chicken Stock (page 20)
250ml dark soy sauce (or light soy sauce if you prefer)
250ml Shaoxing wine
4 cloves garlic, unpeeled but bruised
1 small brown onion, peeled and roughly chopped
5 thick slices ginger, unpeeled
1 cinnamon quill
3 star anise
½ tsp fennel seeds
½ tsp black peppercorns
½ cup caster sugar

Place all the ingredients in a large saucepan and simmer for 30 minutes. Allow to cool, then strain out all the solids.

When you use this liquid for poaching meat or fish, bring it to the boil for a minute or two after you have removed the meat or fish to kill bacteria, strain it, allow to cool, transfer to a freezer-proof container and freeze it until you need to use it again.

TIP
Try to use this master stock once per week to keep it fresh. If you don't use it, at least boil it once a month and return it to the freezer to kill any bacteria. Every few months, add a few more aromatics and spices to keep the fragrance strong.

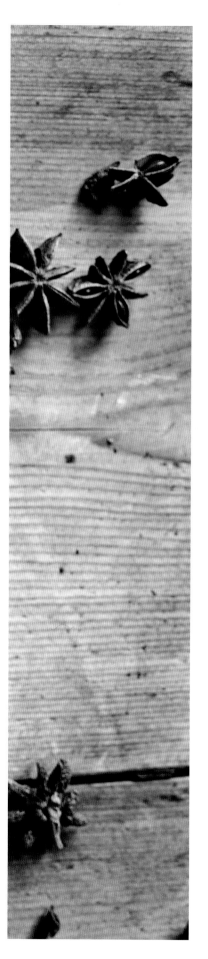

Umami has been around in cookery since antiquity, but the molecules that produce the savoury umami flavour were only formally discovered and named by Professor Kikunae Ikeda in 1908. This all-purpose sauce draws the umami from everyday ingredients and can be used like soy sauce.

UMAMI SAUCE

MAKES: 750 MILLILITRES
PREP: 5 MINUTES / **COOK:** 5 MINUTES

8 dried shiitake mushrooms
100ml mirin
150ml sake
1 tsp caster sugar
500ml light soy sauce
2 tsp fish sauce

Rinse the dried mushrooms quickly under running water to remove any dirt.

Bring the mirin, sake and sugar to the boil in a small saucepan and simmer for 1 minute. Add the soy sauce and fish sauce, bring back to the boil, then add the mushrooms. Remove from the heat and allow to cool. Strain out the mushrooms and transfer the liquid to a bottle (an old soy sauce bottle is perfect). Store in the pantry until ready to use. It will keep for years, and will improve with age.

TIP

This is particularly good as a dipping sauce for sashimi. For an extra umami boost, add a handful of bonito flakes and a 10cm square of kombu seaweed at the same time as the mushrooms, and strain out all the solids before bottling. Keep the mushroom solids for adding to stir-fried dishes, or Cheat's Claypot (page 107).

This simple and clean-tasting Vietnamese pickle is great with grilled meats and rich stews like Caramelised Lemongrass Pork Chops (page 134). You can also add it to salads and sandwiches.

PICKLED CARROT & DAIKON (DO CHUA)

MAKES: 500 GRAMS
PREP: 10 MINUTES / **COOK:** 5 MINUTES / **WAIT:** 30 MINUTES

250ml white vinegar
250ml water
80g caster sugar
½ large daikon (white radish), peeled and cut into
    very thin matchsticks
2 carrots, peeled and cut into very thin matchsticks
2 tsp salt

Mix together the vinegar, water and caster sugar in a small saucepan and stir over medium heat until the sugar is just dissolved. Set aside and allow to cool.

Mix the daikon and carrot with the salt in a large bowl, rubbing the salt into the vegetables with your fingers for a few minutes until each matchstick can be bent so that the ends touch without breaking. Transfer to a sieve and rinse under running water. Drain well.

Place the vegetables in a non-reactive bowl or container and cover with the cooled pickling liquid. Cover and refrigerate for at least 30 minutes before using. The pickles will keep in the liquid for 2–3 weeks.

Making your own sauces is a great way to understand what goes into your food, and teriyaki is an easy place to start. This light version is not as sweet and sticky as many pre-packaged products and can be adjusted to suit your tastes.

LIGHT TERIYAKI

MAKES: ABOUT 700 MILLILITRES
PREP: 5 MINUTES / **COOK:** 2 MINUTES

250ml light soy sauce
200ml mirin
200ml sake
80g caster sugar

Mix together all the ingredients in a small saucepan and stir over low heat until the sugar is just dissolved. Allow to cool. Transfer the sauce to a container and keep in the cupboard until ready to use. I use an old soy sauce bottle or wine bottle, but an ordinary plastic container is fine too.

TIP

A light teriyaki sauce like this isn't just limited to Teriyaki Chicken (page 92). Use it for Beef Bowls (Gyudon) (page 125), as a barbecue marinade or even try adding a tablespoon to give depth to a pot of soup.

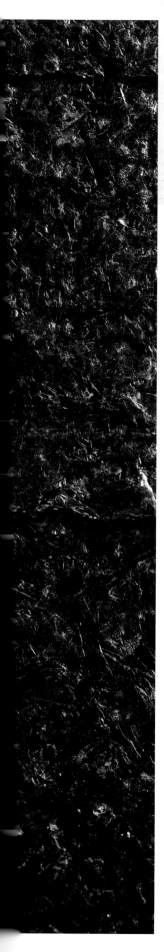

Furikake is a Japanese condiment normally scattered over hot rice. It is versatile and can be used for seasoning dishes like Crispy Squid (page 95), or over salads.

CHILLI FURIKAKE

MAKES: HALF A CUP
PREP: 10 MINUTES

2 sheets nori (see Glossary page 244)
1 tsp white sesame seeds
1 tsp black sesame seeds
5g bonito flakes (about 1 cup large loose flakes)
¼ tsp caster sugar
1 tbsp sea salt flakes
1 tbsp chilli powder

Toast the nori sheets over an open flame for a few seconds until they become brittle and fragrant. (If your nori sheets are pre-toasted you can skip this step.) To toast the sesame seeds, place the white and black seeds in a dry frypan and toss over low heat for a few minutes, or until the white sesame seeds start to turn golden.

Crumble the nori into the bowl of a food processor and process for 2 minutes into small flakes about the size of sesame seeds. Add the bonito flakes and process for another 30 seconds or so, until the bonito flakes reach the same size as the nori flakes. Add the sugar, salt and chilli powder and pulse to combine.

Stir through the toasted sesame seeds. Store in an airtight container in the pantry until you need it. It will keep for months.

TIP
For something different, try sprinkling the furikake over a store-bought roast chicken.

If you can eat Asian food you can cook it. There is no magic nor secret handshake behind it. Asian cuisines strive to draw the best natural flavours from just a few ingredients, judiciously chosen and treated simply.

BALINESE ROAST PORK BELLY WITH FRESH SAMBAL

Due to its predominantly Hindu population, pork is not off the menu in Bali as it is in much of the rest of Muslim Indonesia. Food shows, celebrities and holidaymakers have made the pilgrimage to try Bali's now iconic roast suckling pig - 'babi guling'. This home-style pork roast pays homage to that dish.

SERVES: 6

PREP: 30 MINUTES / **REFRIGERATE:** OVERNIGHT / **COOK:** 70 MINUTES / **REST:** 20 MINUTES

2kg piece pork belly, skin on
2 tbsp cooking salt
Cooked rice, to serve

SPICE PASTE

3 large red or golden shallots, peeled and roughly chopped
4 cloves garlic, peeled
1 thumb-sized knob ginger, peeled
1 large stalk lemongrass, white part only, roughly chopped
1 coriander root, and all stalks attached to it (leaves reserved for garnish)
2 kaffir lime leaves
1 tsp ground turmeric
2 tsp ground coriander
½ tsp caster sugar
¼ tsp ground white pepper
2 tbsp peanut oil, or other vegetable oil
2 tsp fish sauce

FRESH SAMBAL

3 large red or golden shallots, peeled and finely minced
2 large red chillies, finely diced
3 kaffir lime leaves, central vein removed and very finely shredded
1 large stalk lemongrass, white part only, thinly sliced
Juice of 2 limes (about 50ml)
1 tsp white vinegar
½ tsp caster sugar
2 tsp fish sauce
1 tbsp peanut oil, or other vegetable oil

Combine all the ingredients for the spice paste together in a food processor and process to a rough paste.

Prick the pork belly skin all over with a sharp knife or metal skewer, or ask your butcher to score the skin at 1cm intervals. Spread the spice paste generously over the meat side, then rub salt liberally over the skin side. Place on a wire rack on a plate, uncovered, overnight in the fridge to dry the skin and flavour the meat.

Remove the pork from the fridge about 1 hour before roasting. Heat the oven to 190°C (fan-forced, as it gives the best crackling) and roast the pork on a rack for 30 minutes. Reduce the heat to 160°C (fan-forced) and roast for a further 40 minutes, or until the pork is cooked through. If your oven has a grill setting, you can turn this on for the last 10 minutes of cooking to crisp the crackling. Wedging the top of the oven door open a crack with a wooden spoon for this last 10 minutes also allows steam to escape, which will also help the crackling turn crisp. Rest the pork in a draught-free place for at least 20 minutes before carving.

While the pork is cooking, make the fresh sambal by mixing all the sambal ingredients together and allowing to stand for at least 30 minutes before using.

Brush off any excess salt still on the crackling, slice the pork thinly and serve with the fresh sambal and rice.

TIP

Use a teaspoon to peel ginger. The skin comes away very easily, and the spoon can get around the knobs into all the nooks and crannies a peeler can't.

CHICKEN ADOBO

Adobo is the national dish of the Philippines, in which the ingredients are stewed in soy sauce, vinegar and garlic. I love this dish, not just because it's delicious but because it is an authentic Asian dish that can be prepared simply and quickly from readily available ingredients. Isn't that what we're all after?

SERVES: 6
PREP: 10 MINUTES / **MARINATE:** 30 MINUTES / **COOK:** 40 MINUTES

6 chicken marylands (or 2kg chicken wings), skin on
¾ cup dark soy sauce
½ cup white vinegar
6 cloves garlic, peeled and sliced
1 brown onion, peeled and sliced
1 tsp caster sugar
4 bay leaves
1 tsp whole black peppercorns
3 tbsp peanut oil, or other vegetable oil
Steamed rice and greens, to serve

Separate the drumsticks from the marylands, and with a heavy cleaver split the thighs in half across the bone. Alternatively, you can use the marylands whole. If using chicken wings, cut them through the joints, keeping the drumettes and wingettes for this dish, and reserving the wing tips for stock or another purpose.

Combine the chicken with all the remaining ingredients except the oil in a large, non-reactive bowl. Allow to marinate for 30 minutes.

Heat the oil in a large saucepan over high heat until very hot. Remove the chicken from the marinade with tongs and brown it in the hot oil. Pour over the remaining marinade (including the solids), and 1 cup of water, and bring to a simmer. Simmer, covered, for 30 minutes, or until the chicken is very tender.

Allow to cool slightly, uncovered, and serve with steamed rice and greens.

TIP
For something different, substitute half the chicken by weight for skinless pork belly cut into large cubes, and add six whole peeled hard-boiled eggs in the last 10 minutes of cooking.

Brown rice is higher in fibre and protein than white rice, but its firm grains are not to everyone's taste. This rice mixture has a great texture, health benefits and a wonderful nutty flavour. If you choose to add them, the quinoa and sesame seeds add extra taste and texture dimensions again.

TWO-TO-ONE RICE

MAKES: ABOUT 5 CUPS OF COOKED RICE
PREP: 5 MINUTES / **WAIT:** 35 MINUTES / **COOK:** 15 MINUTES

1 cup short- or medium-grain brown rice
1.1 litres water
2 cups short- or medium-grain white rice
2 tbsp quinoa (white, red or black) (optional)
½ tsp toasted sesame seeds
    (white, black or a mixture) (optional)

Wash the brown rice well in a sieve or colander under running water until the water runs clear. Transfer to a medium-sized saucepan, cover with the water and leave to soak for 30 minutes. Wash the white rice and leave in the sieve to drain while the brown rice is soaking.

After 30 minutes, add the white rice to the saucepan and mix well. If using, stir through the quinoa and sesame seeds.

Bring to a simmer over high heat, then reduce the heat and continue to simmer, uncovered, until the water level reaches the top of the rice and tunnels appear where the steam is escaping – about 5 minutes. Cover the saucepan and reduce the heat to very low. Leave for 10 minutes, then turn off the heat. Without removing the lid, allow the rice to stand for a further 5 minutes, then remove the lid and fluff the rice with a rice paddle or wooden spoon. Leave uncovered for 2–3 minutes to allow more steam to escape, then re-cover to keep the rice warm until ready to serve.

TIP
This recipe is in the ratio 2:1 (white:brown), but of course the proportions can be varied to your taste.

LIONS' HEADS

I love the name of this dish, where the meatball is supposed to resemble a lion's head and the soft vegetables around it the mane. Traditionally, four balls are made for this dish, representing luck, prosperity, longevity and happiness. Which one did you get?

SERVES: 4
PREP: 20 MINUTES / **COOK:** 45 MINUTES

8 dried shiitake mushrooms
2 tbsp cornflour
½ Chinese cabbage, cut into 5cm lengths
Vegetable oil for deep-frying or shallow-frying, about 2 litres
500ml White Chicken Stock (page 20)
1 tbsp light soy sauce
1 tbsp Shaoxing wine
¼ tsp caster sugar
2 spring onions, white and green parts, trimmed and sliced, to serve
Cooked rice, to serve

LIONS' HEAD MEATBALLS

750g pork mince
2–3 spring onions, white and light green parts, trimmed and minced
1 tsp grated ginger
1 egg yolk
1 tbsp cornflour
2 tbsp oyster sauce
2 tsp Shaoxing wine
1 tsp soy sauce
1 tsp sesame oil
A pinch of white pepper
A pinch of caster sugar
¼ tsp salt

Rinse the shiitake mushrooms quickly under running water and soak in 1½ cups hot water for at least 20 minutes until softened. Trim and discard the stems, slice the caps, and reserve the liquid.

For the meatballs, mix together all the ingredients and shape into 4 large balls. Sprinkle with the additional 2 tbsp of cornflour to coat, and set aside.

Place the cabbage and shiitake mushrooms in the base of a large casserole dish. Deep- or shallow-fry the meatballs in plenty of oil until well browned all over. Place the meatballs on top of the cabbage and pour over the stock, soy sauce, wine, sugar and the reserved shiitake steeping liquid. Bring to the boil, then reduce the heat and simmer, covered, for about 30 minutes, or until the meatballs are cooked through and the cabbage is very soft. Scatter with spring onions and serve with rice.

TIP
Experiment with adding different ingredients to the meatballs. Chopped water chestnuts, peanuts and dried shrimp all go very well. Alternatively, try using beef instead of pork.

All around the northern parts of China you can buy delicious lamb skewers, rubbed with chilli, cumin and garlic and grilled over hot coals. An easy Sunday roast using these flavours is my favourite way to roast lamb.

NORTHERN CHINESE ROAST LAMB

SERVES: 4–6
PREP: 10 MINUTES / MARINATE: 2 HOURS /
COOK: 1 HOUR 40 MINUTES / REST: 15–30 MINUTES

2kg lamb leg or shoulder roast (bone in)
Cooked rice, to serve

MARINADE
1 large brown onion, peeled and roughly chopped
3 cloves garlic, peeled
1 tsp salt
1 tsp sugar
2 tsp chilli powder
2 tsp ground cumin plus 2 tsp whole cumin seeds
1 tbsp white vinegar
2 tbsp peanut oil
¼ tsp ground black pepper

Purée the onion and garlic in a food processor. Add the remaining marinade ingredients and pulse until well combined.

Score the fat of the lamb and rub the marinade all over the joint. A large Ziploc bag makes this very easy, as you can seal the top and then massage the bag to coat the lamb while keeping your hands clean. Marinate for at least one hour (or overnight if possible). If marinating in the fridge, return the lamb to room temperature for 1 hour before roasting.

Heat the oven to 220°C (fan-forced). Place the lamb in a roasting tray in the oven, immediately reduce the heat to 160°C (fan-forced) and roast for 25 minutes per 500g. Remove from the oven and rest for 15–30 minutes. Serve with rice.

TIP
If you prefer to try this with skewers, leave the onion out of the marinade, rub the other ingredients onto lamb skewers and grill on a barbecue.

PI–PA ROAST DUCK

Roasting a duck is no harder than roasting a chicken, and as whole ducks become more readily available in supermarkets there's no reason not to give it a go. Pi-pa duck is a Cantonese-style roast duck similar in taste to the famous Peking duck, but much easier to make at home from ordinary ingredients. The name comes from the shape of the butterflied duck, which is similar to a Chinese guitar-like instrument called a pi-pa.

SERVES: 4

PREP: 20 MINUTES / **REFRIGERATE:** OVERNIGHT / **COOK:** 90 MINUTES

1 whole duck (about 2kg)

DRYING LACQUER

¼ cup honey
¼ cup Shaoxing wine
2 tbsp white vinegar
½ tsp cooking salt

MEAT RUB

1 tbsp hoisin sauce
2 tsp Chinese five-spice powder

CHILLI IN VINEGAR

4 bird's-eye chillies, roughly chopped
1 clove garlic, peeled and roughly chopped
2 tbsp white vinegar
1½ tsp caster sugar
¼ tsp salt

Remove the wings at the winglet joint (reserving the wingette and wing tip for stock or another purpose), leaving the drumette attached to the duck – i.e. there should be one of the three segments of the wing remaining on the duck.

Mix together the ingredients for the drying lacquer and stir well. In a separate bowl, mix together the ingredients for the meat rub.

Clean the inside of your sink (particularly around the plug hole) with a sponge and hot soapy water and rinse well. Boil a kettle of water and put the whole duck in the sink. Pour the boiling water all over the duck until the skin tightens. Turn it over and repeat. You may need to boil the kettle again for a second round to ensure the skin is well tightened.

Transfer the duck to a cutting board and cut through the breastbone along its entire length. You can do this with a cleaver, a pair of poultry shears or strong kitchen scissors. Turn the duck breast-side down and press firmly to spread it into a butterflied shape. Turn the duck over and brush the cavity side with the meat rub, then transfer to a tray that will fit into your fridge. (Place the duck in the tray skin-side up, then brush the skin with the drying lacquer.) Put in the fridge, uncovered, to dry overnight. Reserve the excess drying lacquer for basting during cooking.

Heat the oven to 180°C (fan-forced) and transfer the duck, skin-side up, to a rack on a roasting tray. Brush the duck skin one more time with the lacquer and roast for 45 minutes. Continue basting the skin with the lacquer every 15 minutes. Reduce the temperature to 140°C (fan-forced) and roast for a further 45 minutes, or until the meat of the duck feels soft around the leg.

While the duck is roasting, mix together all the chilli in vinegar ingredients in a small bowl until the sugar and salt are dissolved.

Slice the duck into portions, lay the portions on a platter and serve with chilli in vinegar (or a little extra hoisin sauce, if you prefer).

TIP

If you don't have time to wait overnight, you can pour the drying lacquer over the duck before cutting, and hang it to dry from string looped under each wing for at least 1 hour in a breezy location (or in front of an electric fan), then butterfly it and brush the meat with the meat rub, roasting as normal.

LECHE FLAN

Leche flan is a dense Filipino crème caramel, and it's one of the easiest desserts you could ever make. Using ingredients from your pantry, the perfect match between the saltiness of the evaporated milk and the sweetness of the condensed milk gives you not just a delicious dessert, but it also paints a fascinating picture of the history of these Western-influenced ingredients in South-East Asia.

SERVES: 6
PREP: 10 MINUTES / **COOK:** 1 HOUR / **REFRIGERATE:** 1 HOUR

½ cup sugar
4 whole eggs plus 2 egg yolks
1 can (375ml) evaporated milk
1 can (395g/300ml) sweetened condensed milk
½ tsp vanilla paste or vanilla extract

Heat the sugar over medium heat in a small saucepan, swirling the saucepan at regular intervals until the sugar liquefies and turns to a golden caramel. (Watch the caramel closely, as it can burn easily. After the sugar has melted, the caramel will change colour quickly, and will continue to darken slightly even after removed from the heat, which will affect both the colour and taste of your flan.) Pour into the base of a 20cm diameter round baking pan and allow to harden for a few minutes at room temperature. There is no need to line or grease the pan.

Whisk together the remaining ingredients and pour through a fine sieve over the caramel to remove any lumps. (Flashing a blowtorch over the top of the mixture at this stage will remove any air bubbles that have risen to the top, but if you don't have one they can be popped with a skewer.)

Put the pan in the basket of a bamboo steamer and steam over medium heat for 30–40 minutes, or until the centre is just barely set (test by tapping or wiggling the tin and watching the ripples on the top of the flan – the ripples will flow less easily the more the flan sets), then remove from the heat. It's best to take the flan off the heat while the centre is still a little wobbly, as it will continue to set.

Allow the flan to cool to room temperature, cover with foil, then refrigerate for at least an hour until chilled and well set. Run a knife or spatula around the edge of the flan and turn it out, upside down, onto a large serving plate. Slice and serve.

TIP

If you prefer to bake this flan, put the pan in a larger baking tray and pour boiling water into the larger tray until it comes halfway up the sides of the leche flan pan. Bake in a 180°C (traditional) oven for about 1 hour, testing for doneness as described above then remove from the oven. If you prefer a richer, more dense flan, substitute 2 egg yolks each for some or all of the whole eggs. The flan can even be made with any ratio of whole eggs to yolks, from 5 whole eggs and no yolks for a lighter flan, to 10 egg yolks and no whites for a flan that is very dense and rich.

ASAMI'S CHEESECAKE

This is my wife's truly amazing Japanese-style baked cheesecake. It's as rich and dense as they come, and it's served in the very Japanese way – sliced into little bars – so you don't have to feel too guilty about having a piece.

MAKES: 1 CHEESECAKE, ABOUT 8–10 SERVES
PREP: 20 MINUTES / **REFRIGERATE:** 30 MINUTES / **COOK:** 75 MINUTES / **STAND:** 3 HOURS / **REFRIGERATE:** OVERNIGHT

BASE
6 wholemeal digestive biscuits
35g unsalted butter
Sea salt, to taste

FILLING
125g sour cream
250g cream cheese
1 egg
50g soft brown sugar
50g caster sugar
100ml thickened cream
1 tsp good-quality dark rum
1 tsp vanilla paste or vanilla extract
2 tbsp cornflour

Line a 10 × 20cm rectangular loaf pan with baking paper. To make the base, put the biscuits in a large bowl and crush with the end of a mallet (or put them in a plastic bag and bash them). Melt the butter and pour into the crushed biscuits. Season with a pinch or two of salt and mix well. (I like the base quite salty to offset the rich filling.) Press the biscuit mix well into the base of the tin (the base should not go up the sides of the tin). Refrigerate for 30 minutes to firm.

Heat the oven to 160°C (fan-forced, or 180°C traditional). In a large bowl, mix together the sour cream and cream cheese with a wooden spoon or spatula. Stir in the egg and sugars, then add the cream, rum and vanilla and fold everything together. Stir in the cornflour (there's no need to sieve it first) and then allow the mixture to drain through a fine sieve (don't push it through or you may get small lumps).

Pour the mixture over the biscuit base in the pan. Tap the pan on the bench firmly a few times to remove any air bubbles. This step is very important, as air bubbles will expand with baking and affect the texture of the filling.

Place the pan in a larger baking tray and fill the large baking tray with boiling water halfway up the sides of the cheesecake pan. Bake the cheesecake for 1¼ hours, or until the top is well browned. Turn off the oven, keeping the door closed, and leave the cheesecake undisturbed for about 3 hours. Removing it from the oven before that time will cool it too quickly and you may get cracks in your filling.

After 3 hours, remove the cheesecake from the oven, cover with foil and refrigerate overnight to allow it to set further. Cut the cheesecake into bars and serve.

TIP
This recipe is for one cheesecake, but I recommend making two at a time (but beat the fillings separately). It's just a little extra effort, but even if you can't eat it yourself, you can give it to someone who will appreciate it.

MONDAY

Back in the 1980s when my dad lived in country South Australia, he served this at a dinner party. Nobody touched it for the first half hour because all his guests thought he'd served ice cream with soy sauce. Our understanding of Asian food in Australia has certainly come a long way since then. If you've never used tofu before because you don't know what to do with it, give this a try - you'll love it.

SOY-DRESSED TOFU

SERVES: 1 (OR MORE AS PART OF A SHARED MEAL)
PREP: 5 MINUTES / **STAND:** 20 MINUTES / **COOK:** 5 MINUTES

1 block (300g) silken tofu
2 tsp peanut oil, or other vegetable oil
½ brown onion, peeled and diced
2 cloves garlic, peeled and roughly chopped
A pinch of salt
A pinch of caster sugar
1 tsp dark soy sauce
1 medium spring onion, white and light green parts,
    trimmed and thinly sliced, to serve

Turn the tofu out onto a double layer of kitchen paper (you may need to run a knife around the edge of the packet). Wrap the tofu, put a plate on top and let it stand for about 20 minutes to press out any excess water. Transfer the tofu to a serving plate.

In a small frypan, heat the oil and fry the onion first, adding the garlic and salt after about 30 seconds. When the onions and garlic are starting to brown, sprinkle over the sugar and continue to fry until the onion and garlic are caramelised in the sugar. Remove the pan from the heat, stir through the dark soy sauce and pour everything over the tofu. Scatter with the spring onion and serve immediately.

TIP
Different varieties of tofu differ in the amount (and sometimes type) of coagulant used by tofu makers. Find a brand and texture you like, although very firm varieties of tofu may be too heavy for this dish.

BANG-BANG CHICKEN SALAD

Bang-bang chicken was so named because the tough chicken breasts were beaten with a stick to separate them into thin shreds.

SERVES: 2 (OR MORE AS PART OF A SHARED MEAL)
PREP: 15 MINUTES / **COOK:** 20 MINUTES

2 small chicken breasts, (or 3 thighs if preferred) skinless and boneless, at room temperature
½ tsp sea salt
1 continental cucumber, peeled, deseeded and cut into thin matchsticks, to serve
2–3 spring onions, white and green parts, trimmed and thinly sliced, to serve

BANG-BANG DRESSING
2 tsp Sichuan peppercorns
⅓ cup white sesame seeds
3 tsp caster sugar
3 tsp Chinkiang black vinegar
3 tsp light soy sauce
2 tsp sesame oil
2 tsp Hot Chilli Oil (page 24), plus extra

To make the dressing, first toast the Sichuan peppercorns and sesame seeds in a dry frypan until the sesame seeds turn golden brown. Transfer to a mortar and grind to a smooth paste. Add the remaining dressing ingredients and combine well.

Place a steamer on top of a large pot or wok of water and bring the water to a simmer. Place the breasts or thighs in the steamer and steam over very low heat for 15–20 minutes, or until just cooked through. Rest for 5 minutes.

With a mallet or the flat side of a heavy knife, bash the chicken a little so that the muscle fibres separate. Sprinkle salt on your hands and tear the chicken into thin shreds. If you prefer, you can just slice the chicken thinly. Toss the dressing through the chicken so it is well coated. Arrange the cucumber on your serving dish, place the chicken on top and scatter with the spring onion. Drizzle with a little extra Hot Chilli Oil and serve.

TIP
If you want to make this a more substantial, meal-sized salad, add some extra salad leaves, sliced radish and cherry tomatoes and toss it all together. For sliced spring onions that curl, cut them into 5cm lengths then split them halfway along their lengths. Open them out so that the layers are flat rectangles, and finely slice them on an angle. Place into cold water to curl.

XO BEEF & BROCCOLI

There is a real art to cooking with a wok, and watching an expert Cantonese chef working his wok station is a sight to behold. To get the best results at home, use a good wok made from carbon steel, cast iron or stainless steel, and season it well (see page 69). Cook over a high gas flame and never overcrowd it. Fry ingredients in batches if necessary to preserve the heat of the wok and to achieve the 'wok hei' (the spirit of the wok) that good wok dishes strive for. Mastery of your wok is the gateway to hundreds of lightning-fast, delicious dishes.

SERVES: 2 (OR MORE AS PART OF A SHARED MEAL)
PREP: 10 MINUTES / **COOK:** 10 MINUTES

350g beef, Scotch fillet, rump or topside, sliced thinly across the grain
200g broccoli, broken into florets
1 tbsp peanut oil, or other vegetable oil
A pinch of sea salt
1 tbsp Liaw Family XO Sauce (page 22)
A pinch of caster sugar
½ tsp cornflour mixed into 2 tbsp White Chicken Stock (page 20), or water

MEAT MARINADE
1 tsp light soy sauce
1 tsp sesame oil
1 tsp Shaoxing wine
½ tsp cornflour

Mix together the beef and the marinade ingredients. Bring some water to the boil in a wok or saucepan and blanch the broccoli for 1 minute, refresh in iced water, and drain.

Heat a wok until very hot and drizzle the oil around the edges. Add the beef, season with a pinch of salt and fry for 1–2 minutes, or until browned. Add in the XO Sauce, broccoli and sugar, and stir-fry for another minute until the meat is well coated. If it starts to look too dry, you can moisten the mixture with a little stock or water.

Drizzle over the cornflour mixture, toss for a further 30 seconds, and transfer to a plate to serve.

TIP
This style of stir-frying has an almost unlimited number of variations. Try substituting sliced chicken thigh or pork neck for the beef, or in-season asparagus for the broccoli.

As kids we would sometimes add a little dollop of butter and soy sauce to our rice for a treat. The flavour combination of the butter, soy sauce and the nuttiness of the toasted rice in these simple grilled rice balls makes for surprisingly satisfying comfort food.

HOT-BUTTERED ONIGIRI

MAKES: 4 ONIGIRI
PREP: 5 MINUTES / **COOK:** 20 MINUTES

2 tsp Chilli Furikake (page 33), optional
3 cups cooked Two-To-One rice (page 40), or cooked
    short- or medium-grain rice
1 tbsp unsalted butter
1 tbsp light soy sauce, or Umami Sauce (page 29)
A pinch of sugar

Mix the Chilli Furikake, if using, through the warm rice. Divide rice into four equal portions (¾ cup of cooked rice each). Wet your hands and mould the rice into your preferred shape. (If you haven't added the Chilli Furikake, sprinkle a little salt onto your hands to flavour the rice as you mould it.) I prefer to make a roughly triangular or a round shape, flattened on the sides so that they lie well under the grill. The rice should be pressed so that it just holds together without being mashed.

Melt the butter in a small saucepan or microwave and mix through the soy or Umami Sauce and the sugar.

Place the rice balls on an oiled wire grill or some baking paper and, with a pastry brush, brush the top of each ball with a little of the butter mixture. Grill for about 10 minutes on one side, brushing twice more with the butter mixture during the grilling, until the top is crispy and golden brown. Turn the rice balls over and repeat the process on the other side. Serve while still warm.

TIP
You can also cook the onigiri in a frypan or on a barbecue grill. Grilling brings out wonderful flavours in soy sauce, so use a good quality brewed soy sauce if you don't have any Umami Sauce.

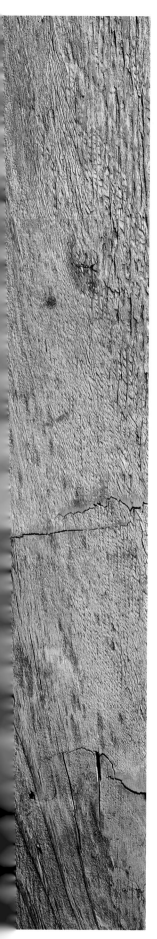

The Australian-Chinese term 'short soup' refers to a clear soup of wontons, and a 'long soup' is a soup of noodles. This soup can be a full dish in itself, or you can halve the recipe to produce a side soup for rice dishes.

SHORT SOUP

SERVES: 4
PREP: 10 MINUTES / **COOK:** 15 MINUTES

1 bunch choy sum
1¼ litres White Chicken Stock (page 20)
3 thick slices ginger, bruised
2 cloves garlic, bruised
½ tsp salt
2 tsp light soy sauce
2 tsp mirin
A pinch of white pepper
1 spring onion, trimmed and thinly sliced
16 Pork & Prawn Wontons (page 214)

Wash the choy sum in running water, being sure to remove any dirt between the stalks at the root.

In a large saucepan, bring the chicken stock, ginger, garlic, salt, soy sauce, mirin, pepper and dark green parts of the spring onion to a low simmer (do not boil), and continue to simmer, covered, for 5 minutes. Remove the ginger, garlic and spring onion tops.

Bring a separate saucepan of water to the boil and season well with salt. Boil the choy sum whole for about 2 minutes until tender, then drain well and slice into 5cm lengths, discarding the root. Boil the wontons for 4 minutes (5 minutes if from frozen), drain and transfer to four individual bowls. Add the choy sum to the bowls, then pour over the hot soup. Scatter sparingly with the remaining spring onions and serve.

TIP

For both long and short soup, you might like to add some boiled thin egg noodles. It's better to boil the wontons and egg noodles separately to the soup; cooking them together will make the soup cloudy and thick.

This is one of those simple, home-style dishes that shows how elegant Asian home cooking can be. Asian food is not always about brash, bold flavours, zing or chilli, and in this case the goal is an impossibly delicate egg custard that looks and feels like silk sheets.

SAVOURY EGG CUSTARD

SERVES: 2 (OR MORE AS PART OF A SHARED MEAL)
PREP: 5 MINUTES / **COOK:** 20 MINUTES

3 eggs
About 350ml White Chicken Stock (page 20),
    or vegetable stock
Salt and white pepper, to season
A dash of sesame oil

Crack the eggs into a 500ml measuring cup. Season the White Chicken Stock with salt, stirring to dissolve until it is as salty as seawater, and add the stock to the eggs to make up a total volume of 500ml. Add in a good pinch of white pepper and a dash of sesame oil.

Carefully mix the eggs and stock mixture together in a larger bowl with a pair of chopsticks, trying not to incorporate too much air into the mixture. Strain the whole mixture through a fine sieve into a heatproof dish.

Place a bamboo steamer over a large pot of water and bring the water to the boil. Reduce the heat to low, put the dish of egg mixture in the steamer and gently steam for about 15 minutes, or until it is set (it will still wobble a little if you tap the dish).

Serve with rice and other meat or vegetable dishes.

TIP
Add 100g minced pork to the egg mixture for a more substantial dish. You will need to slightly reduce the amount of stock used, and steam the mixture slightly longer.

Seasoning creates a natural non-stick coating on your wok. To season a steel wok, rub the inside with paper towel soaked in vegetable oil and place over medium heat for about 10 minutes. It will smoke a lot, so make sure your kitchen is well ventilated. Remove from the heat and wipe well with clean paper towel to remove the black residue. Repeat the oiling, heating and wiping three or four times until there is no more black residue. To keep your wok well seasoned, don't wash it with soap. Just brush it down under running water and dry it back on the stove. Wipe the wok with a thin layer of oil before putting it away.

TEMPURA PUMPKIN & ONION WITH CURRY SALT

The secret to a light and crispy tempura batter is air, water vapour and carbon dioxide. Using sifted self-raising flour and chilled soda water creates lots of these gases, which will try to burst out of the batter as it cooks in the hot oil, leaving you with a light and crispy coating. You can eat tempura with a dipping sauce, but I prefer flavoured salts like this one. When deep-frying, a thermometer is worth the investment as it is a great tool for checking and maintaining oil temperature.

SERVES: 2 (OR MORE AS PART OF A SHARED MEAL)
PREP: 15 MINUTES / **COOK:** 10 MINUTES

¼ Japanese pumpkin (such as the Kent variety)
2 brown onions
2 tsp self-raising flour
Vegetable oil for deep-frying (about 2 litres)

TEMPURA BATTER
1 tbsp cornflour
About 2 cups self-raising flour
1 egg
About 2 cups chilled soda water

CURRY SALT
2 tsp salt
¼ tsp curry powder

To make the tempura batter, take two identically sized bowls or large glasses (about 500ml capacity) and put the cornflour in one, then fill the remainder of the bowl or glass with self-raising flour. In another, crack in the egg and fill to the same level as the flour with chilled soda water. Mix the egg and soda well and sift the flour into a large bowl. Pour over the egg and soda mix and stir gently with a pair of chopsticks. Don't over-mix the batter – a few lumps is completely fine.

For the curry salt, dry-fry the salt in a small frypan for 1–2 minutes until dry. Mix with the curry powder and grind in a mortar and pestle until a smooth powder.

Remove the seeds from the pumpkin and scrub the skin. There is no need to peel it. Slice into thin crescents and place on a tray. Peel and slice the brown onions and place in a bowl.

Sift 1 tsp flour over the pumpkin and stir 1 tsp flour through the onion. Add 2 tbsp tempura batter to the onion and stir to ensure the onion is coated in the batter.

Heat the oil to 165°C in a wide saucepan or wok. Using chopsticks, pick up clumps of the onion mix and drop them into the oil, ensuring the clumps are light but aren't breaking apart. Skim off any small pieces of batter that float away from the onion. Fry for 3–4 minutes, or until just starting to turn golden, and remove to drain on a wire rack.

Dip the pumpkin into the batter and allow the excess to drain off. Add to the oil and fry for 4–5 minutes, or until just starting to turn golden, and drain on a wire rack. Serve the onion and pumpkin with the curry salt.

TIP
The same tempura batter can be used for seafood and other vegetables. If making seafood tempura, fry in 180°C oil, as the seafood inside the batter will cook faster than the vegetables, and the higher temperature is needed to get a crispy coating in a shorter time.

SINGAPORE NOODLES

Don't be fooled by the name – Singapore noodles is actually a contemporary Cantonese dish popularised first in Hong Kong, and then around the world via suburban Cantonese-based Chinese restaurants. The name itself comes from the curry powder in the dish – a nod to the multicultural diversity and Indian influences in much of Singapore's national cuisine.

SERVES: 4

PREP: 15 MINUTES / **SOAK:** 20 MINUTES / **COOK:** 10 MINUTES

200g dried rice vermicelli

2 tbsp peanut oil, or other vegetable oil

150g raw prawns, peeled and deveined

100g char siu pork (available from Chinese barbecue shops), thinly sliced (or substitute sliced pork fillet or chicken breast)

½ red capsicum, deseeded and thinly sliced

2 bunches pak choy, root end removed, cut into 3cm pieces

2–3 spring onions, white and green parts, trimmed and diagonally sliced

A handful (80g) beansprouts

SAUCE

2 tbsp peanut oil, or other vegetable oil

1 tsp grated ginger

3 tbsp curry powder

½ tsp salt

1 tbsp soy sauce

1 tbsp Shaoxing wine

¼ tsp cornflour mixed into ¼ cup White Chicken Stock (page 20), or water

½ tsp caster sugar

Soak the rice vermicelli in warm water for about 20 minutes until the noodles soften and separate. Drain and set aside.

Make the sauce by heating the oil in a wok over medium heat and adding the ginger and curry powder. Fry for just a few seconds, until the curry powder is fragrant but not changing colour, then add the remaining sauce ingredients. Cook for about 1 minute, or until the sauce thickens, then pour into a clean bowl.

Heat the oil in the wok (you don't need to clean it) over medium heat and fry the prawns until they start to change colour. Add the char siu, capsicum, pak choy and spring onions, and stir-fry until the vegetables have softened. Add the noodles and pour over the sauce, tossing to coat the noodles as they cook and soften further for 4–5 minutes. If the noodles are looking too dry, add a little more water or stock. Toss through the beansprouts, fry for another minute to soften them, and serve.

TIP

In their dried form, rice vermicelli and mung bean vermicelli (bean thread noodles) look very similar but will cook quite differently. Make sure you're buying the right kind of noodle.

MISO-ROASTED EGGPLANT

Miso and eggplant are just a fantastic combination. This dish, known in Japan as nasu dengaku, is more traditionally served as a thick miso sauce topping eggplants that have been halved lengthways and grilled. I prefer this version for home cooking, as it suits the larger European eggplants, and the extra roasting of the miso gives a lovely nutty-sweet flavour.

SERVES: 4 (OR MORE AS PART OF A SHARED MEAL)
PREP: 10 MINUTES / **COOK:** 30 MINUTES

2 large eggplants, cut into 2cm cubes
2 tbsp olive oil
Sea salt, to taste
2 spring onions, thinly sliced, to serve
Toasted white and black sesame seeds, to serve

MISO DRESSING
3 tbsp white or red miso
1 tbsp sugar
2 tbsp mirin
1 tbsp sake
2 tbsp water

Heat the oven to 200°C (fan-forced). Toss the eggplant in the olive oil and season with a little salt. Place on a baking tray lined with baking paper and roast for 20 minutes, or until the eggplant is slightly browned. If you like, you can salt and rinse the eggplants first, but it's not really necessary as the bitterness in the eggplant works well with the sweet miso.

Meanwhile, mix together the miso dressing ingredients and pour over the roasted eggplant, tossing it on the tray to coat well. Continue to roast for a further 5–10 minutes, or until the miso sauce starts to caramelise.

Remove the eggplant from the oven, transfer to a serving plate, scatter with spring onion and toasted sesame seeds, and serve.

TIP
To avoid burning black sesame seeds, toast them in a pan with white sesame seeds and watch for the white ones to change colour.

Japanese pickles are a great accompaniment to any rice dish, or as a small plate served as part of a shared meal. Asazuke means a quick or 'shallow' pickle, and this incredibly simple version uses fish sauce in place of kombu seaweed for a hit of umami. Keep some in the fridge to serve as an instant side dish.

ASAZUKE

MAKES: 500 GRAMS
PREP: 10 MINUTES / **REFRIGERATE:** 3 HOURS

300g Chinese cabbage
½ carrot, peeled and thinly sliced into half moons
1 Lebanese cucumber, peeled and cut into
    irregular wedges
½ tsp salt
A few dashes of fish sauce

Wash the cabbage in running water to remove any dirt, and drain well. Cut the leaves in half lengthways and then across into 3cm pieces.

Place the cabbage, carrot and cucumber in a Ziploc bag, add the salt and fish sauce and squeeze as much air out of the bag as possible before sealing it. Massage the bag for about 2 minutes to work the salt and fish sauce into the vegetables. Place the bag in the fridge and leave for around 3 hours. Drain off any accumulated liquid before serving. This pickle will keep in the fridge for about 2 weeks.

TIP
If you prefer, instead of the fish sauce you can add 1 piece of kombu, thinly cut with scissors into ribbons.

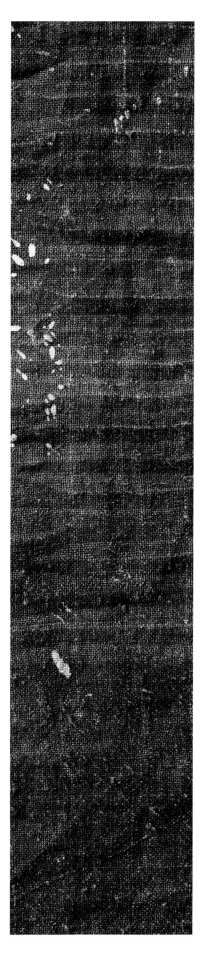

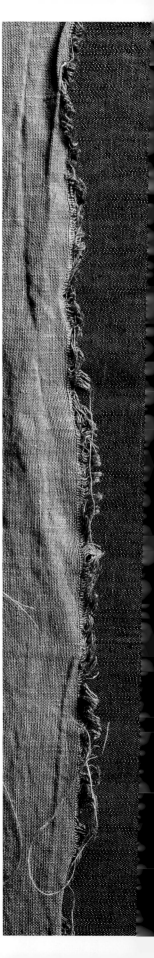

Everybody needs a few really great, simple salad dressings in their repertoire. This one has very little oil and goes wonderfully with Asian foods.

SPINACH & SESAME SALAD

SERVES: 1 (OR MORE AS PART OF A SHARED MEAL)
PREP: 10 MINUTES

2 large handfuls (about 100g) baby spinach leaves
1 Lebanese cucumber, peeled and thinly sliced

SOY & SESAME DRESSING
2 large or 4 small spring onions, white and light
    green parts
1 tbsp light soy sauce
1 tsp caster sugar
2 tbsp rice vinegar or apple cider vinegar
1 tbsp toasted sesame seeds
1 tbsp sesame oil

For the dressing, trim and cut the spring onions in half lengthways and thinly slice. Mix all the dressing ingredients together in a jar, shaking well to dissolve the sugar.

Toss the baby spinach and cucumber on a serving plate, pour over the dressing and serve immediately.

TIP
Dressings like these are magic in the kitchen – you pop everything into a jar, shake it up and you're ready to add flavour to just about anything. This dressing is also great with fried or steamed chicken, or even on grilled pork. Just pour it over the top.

MASTER STOCK POACHED CHICKEN BREAST

This poached chicken is a fast and flavourful way to use your Faster Master during the week. The ginger and spring onion oil is usually served with my family favourite, Hainanese chicken rice, but in this case the pungency and toastiness of the oil works amazingly well with the slightly sweet and fragrant chicken.

SERVES: 2

PREP: 5 MINUTES / **COOK:** 10 MINUTES / **STAND:** 2 MINUTES

---

2 litres Faster Master (page 28)
2 chicken breasts, skinless (about 160g)
A handful of coriander leaves, to serve (optional)
Cooked rice, to serve
Steamed greens, to serve

GINGER & SPRING ONION OIL

2 tbsp grated ginger
4 medium spring onions, white and light green
    parts, trimmed and thinly sliced
½ tsp sea salt
3 tbsp peanut oil, or other vegetable oil

Bring the Faster Master to a simmer in a medium-sized saucepan. Remove from the heat, add the chicken breasts and cover tightly. Allow to stand for 10 minutes, then remove the chicken and let rest for a further 2 minutes.

For the ginger and spring onion oil, pound the ginger, spring onion and salt in a heatproof mortar to a rough paste. Heat the oil in a pan over high heat until smoking hot, then pour onto the mixture. Once the sizzling stops, mix the sauce and allow to stand until ready to serve.

Slice the chicken, scatter with coriander and serve with the ginger and spring onion oil, rice and greens.

TIP

The traditional version of the ginger and spring onion oil is made with rendered chicken fat. If you have any chicken fat around, or sauce left over from making stock or Chicken Fat Noodles (page 141), substitute it for some of the peanut oil in this recipe.

In Vietnam, an iced coffee is made by drip-filtering coffee through a small metal filter onto condensed milk, then pouring over ice in a tall glass. This affogato version turns the condensed milk into one of the easiest homemade ice creams ever - and you don't even need an ice cream machine.

VIETNAMESE AFFOGATO

MAKES: 1½ LITRES OF ICE CREAM
PREP: 5 MINUTES / **FREEZE:** 4 HOURS

1–2 shots of strong Vietnamese coffee per person
(or substitute espresso)

CONDENSED MILK ICE CREAM
1 can (395g) sweetened condensed milk
600ml thickened cream

To make the ice cream, pour the condensed milk and cream into the bowl of an electric mixer and whip to stiff peaks. Transfer to a container and freeze for at least 4 hours, or until firm.

Place a large scoop of the ice cream in a chilled glass and serve with a shot of Vietnamese coffee in a glass on the side. Pour the coffee over the ice cream and eat immediately with a spoon.

TIP
Adding a shot of Frangelico or other liqueur would make this a sophisticated adult dessert. If you don't want this as an affogato, you can just shake the coffee and a little condensed milk with ice in a cocktail shaker for a delicious short iced coffee.

TUESDAY

This dish is ready in the blink of an eye and really drills home the benefits of having a good XO sauce in the fridge. If a restaurant-quality dish in just a few minutes is the Holy Grail of home cooking, this might well be it.

XO PRAWNS & SNOW PEAS

SERVES: 2 (OR MORE AS PART OF A SHARED MEAL)
PREP: 10 MINUTES / **COOK:** 5 MINUTES

12 large raw prawns, peeled and deveined
1 tsp peanut oil, or other vegetable oil
A pinch of sea salt
10 snow peas, topped and tailed with threads
    removed, sliced in half diagonally
1–2 tbsp Liaw Family XO Sauce (page 22)
½ tsp cornflour mixed into 2 tbsp White Chicken
    Stock (page 20), or water

Butterfly the prawns by cutting through the back about halfway through and pressing open with the flat of a knife.

Heat a wok until very hot and drizzle the oil around the edge. Add the prawns, season with a pinch of salt and fry for about 30 seconds, or until the prawns start to change colour. Add the snow peas and stir-fry for a further minute. Add the Liaw Family XO Sauce and toss through for another minute or so, until the prawns are just cooked and the snow peas are tender but still crunchy. Drizzle over the cornflour mixture a little at a time while tossing for a further 30 seconds, and transfer to a plate to serve.

TIP
Butterflying the prawns may seem unnecessary, but the light and crunchy texture it gives to them is certainly worth the 5 minutes of effort.

'NO. 88' SPECIAL FRIED RICE

SERVES: 4
PREP: 15 MINUTES / **COOK:** 5 MINUTES

I've never known why Chinese restaurants describe their fried rice as 'special', but in most Asian families, fried rice is a meal in itself, not used as a substitute for ordinary steamed rice. All the ingredients for this recipe are pantry staples or keep well in the freezer, so it's a great standby recipe for when you come back from a weekend away, or you haven't been to the shops in a while. For some reason, ever since I was a kid I've always eaten fried rice with a little dollop of tomato sauce. Don't knock it 'til you've tried it!

2 tbsp peanut oil, or other vegetable oil
½ brown onion, peeled and sliced
2 cloves garlic, peeled and roughly chopped
1 tsp sea salt
150g raw prawns, peeled, deveined and split completely in half lengthways
2 Chinese sausages (lap cheong), thinly sliced on the diagonal, or 100g char siu pork (available from Chinese barbecue shops), diced
1 carrot, diced
½ cup frozen peas
2 eggs
6 cups cooked rice
A pinch of white pepper
1 tbsp light soy sauce
1 tbsp dark soy sauce

Heat a wok over medium heat, drizzle in 1 tbsp of the oil and add the onions and then the garlic. Season with a little of the salt and fry until the garlic starts to brown. Add the prawns and Chinese sausage and toss for about 30 seconds, then add in the carrot and peas. Continue to toss for another 1–2 minutes, or until the vegetables start to soften.

Move the contents of the wok to one side of it, add the remaining tablespoon of oil to the open side and crack in the eggs. Move the eggs around to break up the yolks and when they are just starting to set, combine the eggs with the other wok ingredients. Add the rice, and toss to combine all ingredients, pressing the rice against the edges of the wok to break up any clumps. Add the rest of the salt, pepper and soy sauces and fry until the rice is warmed through and free of clumps. Taste and adjust seasoning, and serve.

TIP

Many people prefer to make fried rice with rice cooked the day before, because it is drier and firmer. It's fine to use freshly cooked rice instead, but you will need to be careful not to mash the grains – perhaps add a little extra oil to keep them separate.

HAILAM NOODLES

This noodle dish is a favourite at Hainanese coffee shops all over Malaysia. My grandmother makes a great Hailam Noodles, and she says the secret is in creating a flavourful sauce from the meats and vegetables in the wok for the noodles to soak up as they cook.

SERVES: 4
PREP: 10 MINUTES / **COOK:** 10 MINUTES

1kg fresh Hokkien noodles
300g skinless chicken thighs, thinly sliced
2 tbsp peanut oil, or other vegetable oil
2 thick slices ginger, bruised
3 cloves garlic, peeled and roughly chopped
100g raw prawns, peeled and deveined
2–3 large leaves of Chinese cabbage, sliced
½ carrot, cut into matchsticks
1 tsp cornflour mixed into 1 tbsp cold water
A handful of coriander leaves, to serve
Lime wedges, to serve
Soy sauce and sliced red chillies, to serve

MARINADE

1 tsp soy sauce
1 tsp Shaoxing wine
1 tsp cornflour
½ tsp sesame oil

SAUCE

1 tbsp oyster sauce
1 tsp light soy sauce
¼ tsp ground white pepper
1 tsp Cheong Chan caramel sauce, kecap manis
    or dark soy sauce
A pinch of caster sugar
1 cup White Chicken Stock (page 20)

Pour warm water over the egg noodles, soak for a few minutes, drain and separate carefully. (Don't worry if the noodles are too closely packed to separate – they will come apart as they cook in the wok.) Combine the marinade ingredients and stir through the chicken.

Heat a wok until very hot and drizzle the oil around the edge. Add the ginger, then after a few seconds the garlic. Toss around in the oil until the garlic starts to brown, then add the chicken and stir-fry until it starts to brown. Add the prawns, cabbage, carrot and sauce ingredients except the chicken stock. When the vegetables soften, add the stock and bring to the boil. Taste the sauce; it should be strong and flavourful. You may need to add a little salt.

Add the noodles and stir to combine. Cook for about 2–3 minutes, or until the noodles are nearly al dente. Pour over the cornflour mixture, stir-fry for a further 30 seconds and remove from the heat. Allow to stand for a few moments, then transfer to a plate, garnish with coriander and serve with lime and sliced chillies soaking in a little soy sauce.

TIP

These noodles are excellent with sliced pork, or pork or beef mince. You can also substitute the Hokkien noodles for dried rice vermicelli soaked in warm water.

As popular as it is in the West – and it is one of my favourites – it may surprise you to know that teriyaki chicken as a dish doesn't really exist in Japan. Teriyaki glazes are used mainly for fish; but if it tastes this good, it doesn't need to be traditional.

TERIYAKI CHICKEN

SERVES: 2 (OR MORE AS PART OF A SHARED MEAL)
PREP: 10 MINUTES / **COOK:** 5 MINUTES

3 chicken thighs, skinless
1 tsp cornflour
1 tsp peanut oil
¼ cup Light Teriyaki (page 32)
2 shiso leaves, shredded, or ½ tsp grated ginger,
    to serve (optional)
Japanese mayonnaise, to serve

Slice the chicken thighs into thin medallions and toss with the cornflour to just coat. In a non-stick frypan, heat the oil over high heat and fry the chicken, turning frequently until just browned on all sides but not yet cooked through. Add the Light Teriyaki and toss the chicken to coat in the glaze as it thickens. Remove the chicken from the pan just before it is cooked, and rest for a few minutes to allow to cook through.

Top with some shredded shiso leaves or grated ginger, if you like, and serve with Japanese mayonnaise.

TIP
Shiso, also known as perilla, is an Asian herb with a unique peppery, minty flavour. It's available in Australia from Asian grocery stores, but if you can't find it don't worry – just leave it out.

Salt and pepper squid is an Australian classic, but this version has a little Japanese accent. Rather than messing around with batters or egg whites, a light dusting of rice flour or cornflour is all you need for perfect crispy squid every time.

CRISPY SQUID WITH CHILLI FURIKAKE

SERVES: 2 (OR MORE AS PART OF A SHARED MEAL)
PREP: 10 MINUTES / **COOK:** 5 MINUTES

Vegetable oil for deep-frying (about 2 litres)
500g squid, cleaned and cut into 5mm-wide strips
3 tbsp rice flour or cornflour
2 tbsp Chilli Furikake (page 33)
Freshly ground black pepper, to taste
Lime or lemon wedges, to serve

Heat the oil to 180°C in a deep-fryer, wide saucepan or wok. Toss the squid with the flour to coat. Shake off any excess flour and deep-fry in batches for about 30 seconds to 1 minute, or until just cooked. Use wooden chopsticks to push the squid apart if it is sticking together. Drain well on a wire rack.

Transfer the squid to a serving plate and scatter with the Chilli Furikake and a grind or two of black pepper. Serve with lime or lemon wedges.

TIP
If ordinary salt and pepper squid is more your thing, try using the salt and pepper mix from the Salt & Pepper Pork Belly recipe on page 102.

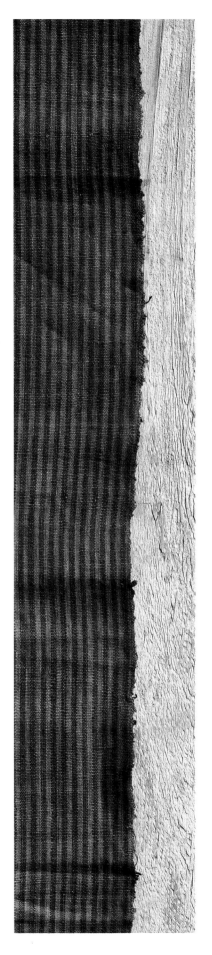

MILLE-FEUILLE WITH CHILLI PONZU

Despite the French name, this fantastic winter one-pot dish is very popular in Japan. It's one of my favourites – I eat it at least once a week in the colder months. Dip the pork and cabbage into the chilli ponzu, but don't forget to drink the soup that forms in the cooking process.

SERVES: 2
PREP: 15 MINUTES / **COOK:** 45 MINUTES

600g piece pork belly, skin and bone removed
½ head of Chinese cabbage
1 tbsp sea salt
¼ tsp ground white pepper
1 tbsp sake
1 tbsp mirin
1 tsp soy sauce

CHILLI PONZU

3 bird's-eye chillies (or to taste), thinly sliced
4 tbsp Fish Sauce Ponzu (page 25)

Slice the pork belly into very thin, long strips, about the thickness of bacon. You can ask your butcher to do this for you, but if you're doing it yourself, freezing the pork for about 30 minutes before you start will make it easier to cut. Separate the leaves of the Chinese cabbage. Mix together the salt and white pepper.

Place a large leaf of cabbage on a clean cutting board and add two or three strips of pork on top. Sprinkle with a little of the salt and pepper mix – you don't need to cover all of the cabbage leaf. Place another cabbage leaf over the pork in the opposite direction (the leafy end should be over the stem end of the bottom leaf), then add 2–3 strips of pork and scatter with a little more of the salt and pepper mix. Repeat the process, alternating the direction of the cabbage leaves, pressing down gently, and using more leaves per layer for the smaller leaves. You should end up with a large, even block of layered cabbage and pork (see pages 98–99).

Cut the block into equal thirds crossways and pack the thirds into a heavy-based lidded casserole dish – cast iron is perfect. Mix together the sake, mirin and soy then pour over the contents of the dish. A little ponzu or unsalted chicken stock works fine too, as an alternative.

Place the casserole dish, lid on, over high heat on the stove top for 1 minute to heat the pot. Then reduce the heat to low and cook for 45 minutes without removing the lid.

For the chilli ponzu, mix the chillies with the ponzu. Serve in individual bowls as a dipping sauce with the mille-feuille.

TIP
For a variation to this dish, add thinly sliced spring onions on top of the pork in every second layer.

PRAWN & AVOCADO DORIA

A doria is a kind of rice-based gratin that apparently originated in France in the early 1900s as a homage to the colours of the Italian flag, and soon became popular in Japan. Doria is almost unheard of in the West now, but in Japan it's still going strong.

SERVES: 2
PREP: 15 MINUTES / **COOK:** 30 MINUTES

2 cloves garlic, peeled and finely chopped
12 raw prawns, peeled and deveined
Salt, to taste
1 tsp brandy
A handful of cherry tomatoes, halved
½ avocado, cut into 1cm cubes
4 cups cooked short-grain rice

ENRICHED BÉCHAMEL

½ onion, peeled and studded with 6 cloves
1 bay leaf
500ml full-cream milk
75g butter, plus 20g extra
2 tbsp plain flour
1 egg yolk
Salt, to taste
A pinch of freshly ground nutmeg

To make the enriched béchamel, place the onion, bay leaf and milk in a small saucepan and bring to the boil. Remove from the heat and set aside to infuse.

Heat the butter and flour in another small saucepan, stirring constantly with a wooden spoon or whisk until it starts to bubble but has not yet turned brown. Add the infused milk in a thin stream, stirring constantly to remove any lumps. Continue to cook for about 5 minutes, stirring constantly until a thick sauce is produced. Remove from the heat (it will continue to thicken off the heat), stir through the egg yolk and season with salt and nutmeg.

Remove the cloves from the onion and finely chop the onion. In a large frypan, heat the additional 20g butter and fry the garlic and onion until softened and the onion is translucent. Add the prawns, season with salt and cook for 2–3 minutes, or until the prawns are almost cooked through. Flambé with brandy and remove from the heat. Stir through the tomato and avocado.

Spread the cooked rice evenly into the base of a heatproof gratin dish and season well with salt. Pour the prawn mixture and any pan juices on top of the rice. Top with an even layer of the béchamel sauce and blowtorch or grill under an overhead grill until the top is browned. Serve immediately.

TIP

The flambé process only burns off about 25 per cent of the alcohol in the brandy, so if you want to avoid alcohol altogether you should skip this step. This recipe can easily be doubled or multiplied to feed a crowd.

Pork belly doesn't always have to be about slow cooking or crispy crackling, and this dish shows just how versatile the cut can be. The secret to a good 'salt and pepper' dish is in the seasoning – too little and it's bland, but too much and that's all you'll taste. If in doubt, add your salt little by little and taste as you go.

SALT & PEPPER PORK BELLY

SERVES: 4
PREP: 10 MINUTES / **COOK:** 5 MINUTES

500g piece pork belly, skin and bones removed
1 tsp sesame oil
2 cloves garlic, peeled and roughly chopped
1 bird's-eye chilli, sliced
2 spring onions, white and light green parts, trimmed
    and sliced
1 tsp salt flakes
¼ tsp freshly ground black pepper
A handful of coriander leaves, to serve

Slice the pork into 1cm steaks, then cut into 3cm squares about 1cm thick.

Heat a wok or large frypan until very hot and add the sesame oil. Fry the pork in batches until well browned on all sides and cooked through. Set aside.

Pour out any excess fat from the pan and add the garlic, chilli and spring onion. Toss over very high heat until the garlic starts to brown and the mixture is very fragrant. Return the pork pieces to the wok, add the salt and black pepper and toss to coat well. Transfer to a warm plate, scatter with coriander leaves and serve.

TIP
Try this salt and pepper mix with prawns in their shell or with deep-fried squid.

One of the most charming truths about cooking is that anyone can do it. It doesn't take unique talent to put something in a saucepan and then take it out again, or to follow a set of instructions in a recipe.

CHEAT'S CLAYPOT

Claypot rice is one of my favourite dishes, but some people struggle with balancing the liquid released by the ingredients and the liquid needed to cook the rice. This 'cheat's' recipe avoids this problem, producing a dish that's ready in minutes and tastes amazing.

SERVES: 4

PREP: 10 MINUTES / **MARINATE:** 10 MINUTES / **COOK:** 10 MINUTES

4 chicken thighs, skinless, sliced
2 Chinese sausages (lap cheong), sliced
8 dried shiitake mushrooms, soaked in 2 cups hot water, stems removed and sliced (liquid reserved)
6 cups warm, cooked white rice
Sea salt, to taste
¼ cup thinly sliced spring onions
A handful coriander leaves, to serve
Chilli sauce, to serve

BASE MARINADE
1 tsp sesame oil
1 tbsp oyster sauce
1 tbsp dark soy sauce
1 tsp Cheong Chan caramel sauce, or dark soy sauce
1 tsp cornflour
¼ tsp sugar
1 tsp Shaoxing wine
2 tsp grated ginger

Mix together all the ingredients for the base marinade and marinate the chicken, sausage and mushrooms for about 10 minutes.

Heat ½ cup of the reserved shiitake mushroom steeping liquid in a large saucepan or claypot and add the chicken, sausage and mushrooms along with the marinade. Stir over high heat until the chicken is cooked through. Add the rice and stir until well combined. Reduce the heat to medium and cook for 5 minutes without stirring, until the rice forms a bit of a crust around the edges of the pot. Season with salt and toss through the spring onions. Garnish with plenty of coriander and serve with chilli sauce.

TIP
To add even more flavour to the dish, cook the rice in White Chicken Stock (page 20) instead of water.

KOREAN PORK & KIMCHI CASSEROLE (KIMCHI CHIGAE)

Known as 'kimchi chigae', this dish really illustrates how Asian home cooking is no more difficult than Western home cooking – it's just that some of the ingredients may be different. This is a great one-pot dish where you can just chuck everything in and it's ready in less than an hour. It's perfect for a cold winter's night.

SERVES: 4
PREP: 25 MINUTES / **COOK:** 30 MINUTES

1 block (300g) silken tofu
6 thick spring onions (or 12 thin), white and
    green parts
180g enoki mushrooms
1 tbsp sesame oil
600g piece pork belly, skin and bone removed,
    cut into 2cm pieces
2 cloves garlic, peeled and minced
1 tsp grated ginger
2 tbsp light soy sauce
2 tbsp sake
2 tbsp Korean chilli-bean paste (gochujang)
1 tsp caster sugar
400g kimchi (drained, with any juice reserved)
750ml White Chicken Stock (page 20), or water
Cooked rice, to serve

Turn the tofu out onto a double layer of kitchen paper (you may need to run a knife around the edge of the packet). Wrap the tofu, put a plate on top and let it stand for about 20 minutes to press out any excess water. Cut into 3cm cubes.

Slice the spring onions on a sharp diagonal angle into 3cm lengths. Break apart the bunch of enoki mushrooms into small clumps, trimming off any dirty bases from the stems.

Heat the sesame oil in a large saucepan over high heat and fry the pork belly for 1–2 minutes, or until the pork is starting to brown. Add the garlic and ginger and fry until fragrant. Add the soy sauce, sake, gochujang and sugar and stir to coat the pork. Add the kimchi (reserving the juice), spring onions and mushrooms and continue to fry for another minute or so. Add the chicken stock or water and kimchi juice, bring to a simmer and continue to simmer, covered, for 10 minutes.

Stir, then place the tofu on top and simmer, covered, for a further 15–20 minutes, or until the pork is just tender.

Since different batches of kimchi may vary in spiciness, saltiness and sweetness, before serving adjust the seasoning of your dish to your taste with chilli powder, chilli oil, salt or sugar if necessary. Serve piping hot with some steamed rice.

TIP
Try this with sliced chicken thigh instead of pork, if you prefer. If you want a milder version, replace some of the kimchi with chopped Chinese cabbage. If you want it a bit hotter, add a teaspoon of chilli powder at the same time as the soy sauce.

There is a lightness to Japanese salads that makes them perfect for summer. They tend to only use minimal oil (if any at all) – teaming a delicious ponzu-based dressing, for example, with fresh flavours. Rather than a meal in itself, a salad like this one is a great accompaniment to grilled or fried dishes.

JAPANESE TOFU SALAD

SERVES: 1 (OR MORE AS PART OF A SHARED MEAL)
PREP: 5 MINUTES / **STAND:** 20 MINUTES

1 block (300g) silken tofu
2 cups loosely packed mixed baby salad leaves, washed and drained
½ cup halved cherry tomatoes
½ tsp Chilli Furikake (page 33) (optional)

DRESSING
2 tbsp Fish Sauce Ponzu (page 25)
2 tsp vegetable oil
½ tsp grated ginger

Turn the tofu out onto a double layer of kitchen paper (you may need to run a knife around the edge of the packet). Wrap the tofu, put a plate on top and let it stand for about 20 minutes to press out any excess water. Cut the tofu into 5cm cubes.

For the dressing, whisk the ingredients together until slightly emulsified.

Toss half of the dressing through the salad leaves and cherry tomatoes and place them on a serving plate. Place the cubes of tofu on top and pour over the remaining dressing. Scatter with the Chilli Furikake if you like, and serve.

TIP
If you prefer, you can leave out the oil for a dressing that is completely fat free.

This hot version of a simple Korean vegetable side dish is great with almost any meal. It keeps for about a week in the fridge, so make a big batch at the start of the week and use it as a side or topping for soups, salads, rice dishes or anything else.

SPICY BEANSPROUT SALAD

SERVE: AS PART OF A SHARED MEAL
PREP: 5 MINUTES / **COOK:** 1 MINUTE / **STAND:** 2 MINUTES

2 cloves garlic, peeled
A pinch of salt flakes
1 tbsp light soy sauce
1 tbsp sesame oil
½ tsp Korean chilli-bean paste (gochujang) (optional)
¼ tsp chilli powder
250g beansprouts, rinsed and drained

Finely chop the garlic, add the salt and, with the flat of the tip of your knife, mash into a paste. Put in a bowl with the remaining ingredients, except the beansprouts, and mix well.

Bring a large pot of water to a vigorous boil. Add the beansprouts for only 45 seconds (the water will stop boiling but you need to time 45 seconds from the moment the beansprouts go into the water, not from when it comes back to the boil). Drain very well. Add the hot beansprouts to the bowl and mix well. Allow to cool to room temperature (or to fridge temperature if preferred), then serve.

CHICKEN WITH GARLIC & CRISPY LIME LEAVES

I love the contrasting textures in this dish – the crunch of the lime leaves and garlic with the succulent, juicy chicken. Be warned, though, this is definitely one for garlic lovers!

SERVES: 2–4 (OR MORE AS PART OF A SHARED MEAL)
PREP: 5 MINUTES / **MARINATE:** 10 MINUTES / **COOK:** 10 MINUTES

4 chicken thighs, skinless
8 cloves garlic, peeled and roughly chopped
10 kaffir lime leaves, veins removed and shredded
Vegetable oil for deep-frying (about 2 litres)
Lime wedges, to serve

MARINADE

1 tbsp fish sauce
2 tsp oyster sauce
½ tsp caster sugar
1 tbsp cornflour
1 tsp sesame oil

Trim any visible fat from the chicken and cut each thigh across the grain into 1cm strips. Mix together all of the marinade ingredients and stir through the chicken strips. Set aside for at least 10 minutes at room temperature.

Heat the oil in a deep-fryer, wok or wide saucepan to 190°C and deep-fry the chicken strips in small batches for 2 minutes, or until well browned and almost cooked. Set aside on a wire rack to drain and rest for a few minutes (the chicken will continue to cook through while resting).

Reduce the heat of the oil to 160°C by adding a little cold oil and testing the temperature again with a thermometer. Fry the garlic until just browned, then scoop out with a wire-mesh strainer, and set aside. Add the shredded lime leaves to the hot oil for just 1–2 seconds until they crisp. Set aside to drain on kitchen paper.

Place the chicken on a warmed plate and scatter the crispy garlic and lime leaves on top. Serve with lime wedges.

TIP

A wok is a great tool for deep- or shallow-frying. Remove oil to raise the temperature more quickly, or add a little cold oil to cool things down.

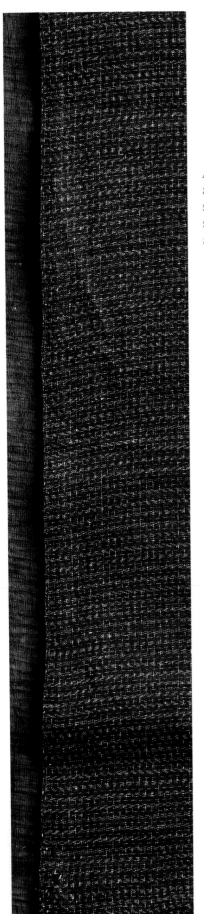

An ideal mid-week dessert is simple, light and sweet without making you feel too guilty, so this granita is just about perfect. Keep some granita base in the freezer all summer and just scrape off a serving as you need it.

LYCHEE & COCONUT GRANITA

MAKES: ABOUT 1 LITRE OF GRANITA BASE
PREP: 5 MINUTES / **FREEZE:** OVERNIGHT

1 can (565g) lychees in syrup
1 can (400ml) coconut milk
1 large pinch sea salt

Place the lychees and their syrup in a blender and blend to a rough purée. Pour in the entire can of coconut milk and a good pinch of salt and pulse until combined.

Churn in an ice cream maker according to manufacturer's instructions, then freeze in a large container overnight until it is set. Churning will give you a lighter granita. If you don't have an ice cream maker, put the mixture in a freezer-proof bowl or tray and freeze as is, whisking for a few seconds every 30 minutes or so to break up the ice crystals until it is set too firm to whisk. When set firm, leave in the freezer until ready to use.

Scrape the set mass with a fork to create a light, fluffy granita and serve in chilled glasses or bowls.

TIP
This is delicious as it is, but if you want something a little more impressive, set your favourite jelly in individual moulds and serve with the granita over the top. It is also a great topping for a tropical fruit salad. Make the granita at least a day in advance, as it will need to be quite firm to scrape.

WEDNESDAY

JAPANESE TRIPLE-FRIED CHICKEN (KARA AGE)

This kind of fried chicken is known in Japan as 'kara age'. My method of triple-frying in hot oil produces a lovely golden-brown, crispy skin and coating from the direct heat of the oil, but the meat of the chicken cooks with residual heat, leaving it more moist and tender than you could ever imagine.

SERVES: 2–4 (OR MORE AS PART OF A SHARED MEAL)
PREP: 10 MINUTES / **MARINATE:** 15 MINUTES / **COOK:** 5 MINUTES

400g chicken thighs, skin on
2 tbsp light soy sauce
1 tbsp sake
1 tsp grated ginger
A pinch of sugar
½ cup potato flour or cornflour, for dusting
A pinch of salt
Vegetable oil for deep-frying (about 2 litres)
Lemon wedges, to serve
Japanese mayonnaise, to serve

Cut the chicken thighs into quarters or large pieces, about 5cm square, and transfer to a non-reactive bowl. Combine the soy sauce, sake, ginger and sugar and marinate the chicken for about 15 minutes.

Place the flour in a large bowl and stir through the salt. Pull the chicken out of the marinade with chopsticks, one piece at a time, and drop into the flour. (Adding the pieces one at a time drains off the marinade, stopping the chicken pieces from sticking together in the flour.) Remove the coated chicken from the flour to a plate or tray and allow to stand uncovered at room temperature for a few minutes. (This helps the flour stick to the chicken and also helps give a crispier coating after frying.)

In a large saucepan or wok, heat the oil to 190°C. Deep-fry the chicken for 1 minute. If you only have a small saucepan, fry in batches to avoid reducing the temperature of the oil too much (place the cooked chicken in a warm oven while cooking the next batch). Remove the chicken and place on a rack over a tray to drain and rest for 30 seconds, then place the chicken back in the oil and fry again for 30 seconds, and then rest on a rack for 30 seconds. Transfer the chicken back to the oil for one last blast of 30 seconds and then drain and rest for 2 minutes. Serve with a wedge of lemon and a little Japanese mayonnaise.

TIP

Draining on a rack instead of paper allows the air to circulate and keeps the chicken crispy. You can substitute the soy sauce and sake with 4 tbsp Umami Sauce (page 29) and, if you prefer, use breast meat (skin on) or wings instead of thighs.

DRY WONTON NOODLES

Rather than in a soup or stir-fry, dressing warm, cooked noodles is a great way to eat them. The flavours of the noodle sauce and Garlic & Shallot Oil match really well, so you might want to make them in big quantities so they are always on hand.

SERVES: 4
PREP: 10 MINUTES / **COOK:** 10 MINUTES

Salt, to taste
1 tsp peanut oil, or other vegetable oil
1 bunch choy sum or gai lan, washed well
A handful beansprouts
12 Pork and Prawn Wontons (page 214)
4 cups fresh thin egg noodles
4 tbsp Garlic & Shallot Oil (page 21)
250g char siu pork (available from
    Chinese barbecue shops), sliced
Spring onion, to garnish
Soy sauce and sliced red chillies, to serve
    (optional)

NOODLE SAUCE
1 tsp caster sugar
1 tbsp oyster sauce
2 tbsp light soy sauce
1 tbsp dark soy sauce

Combine the noodle sauce ingredients and mix well. If the sugar does not dissolve completely, heat the sauce briefly in a small saucepan or in the microwave, but do not bring to the boil.

Bring 3–4 litres of water to a rolling boil in a large saucepan and season with salt. Add the oil to the water. Boil the choy sum or gai lan for about 1 minute, until tender, then drain well and slice into 5cm lengths, discarding the root end. Blanch the beansprouts for 30 seconds, drain and set aside. Boil the wontons for 4 minutes (5 minutes if from frozen), drain and set aside.

Boil the noodles in individual serves for 1 minute each, or until al dente. Drain well and transfer to a large bowl. Toss each serve of noodles together with a few beansprouts and a tablespoon each of the prepared Noodle Sauce and the Garlic & Shallot Oil.

Transfer the noodles to a plate and top with a few slices of char siu, the wontons and some greens. Serve with a garnish of spring onion and sliced red chillies in a little soy sauce if you like.

TIP
You can also serve green chillies pickled in the same pickling liquor as for Pickled Carrot & Daikon (page 30) and some Hot Chilli Oil (page 24). Alternatively, top the noodles with the char siu only, and serve a small bowl of Short Soup (page 65) on the side. If you can't get to a Chinese barbecue shop and you don't want to make your own char siu, substitute some chicken poached in Faster Master stock (page 28), or just leave it out of the recipe.

Gyudon is the ubiquitous Japanese beef rice bowl, found all over Japan (and the rest of the world). You can buy a bowl of gyudon in Japan for as little as two dollars, but made at home this recipe is super-fast and nearly foolproof.

BEEF BOWLS (GYUDON)

SERVES: 4

PREP: 5 MINUTES / **COOK:** 5 MINUTES

¾ cup White Chicken Stock (page 20), or dashi stock
    (available in powdered form)
¾ cup Light Teriyaki (page 32)
1 brown onion, peeled and thickly sliced
500g beef, Scotch fillet, topside or rump, very thinly sliced
6–8 cups cooked short-grain rice, to serve
Chilli powder or Chilli Furikake (page 33), to serve
    (optional)
Japanese red pickled ginger (benishouga), to serve

Bring the White Chicken Stock and Light Teriyaki to the boil together in a medium-sized saucepan. Add the onion and simmer for 2–3 minutes, until the onion has softened. Add the beef and stir until it is just cooked. Taste and season with salt if necessary.

Divide the rice equally between four bowls and top with the beef mixture, allowing a little of the stock to soak into the rice. Sprinkle over a little chilli powder or Chilli Furikake if you like, and serve with pickled ginger.

TIP

To slice the meat very thinly, it helps to place it in the freezer for 1–2 hours beforehand, until quite firm. Use a very sharp knife. Alternatively, thinly sliced beef can be bought from Asian butchers and grocers. You can also try this recipe with very thinly sliced pork. In Japan you can have a range of extra toppings on your gyudon, like soft-boiled eggs, grated radish or even kimchi. Try adding some of your own toppings and see what you like.

FISH SAUCE ROAST CHICKEN

If you're a bit tired of the same old roast chicken, the sticky Thai flavours in this version will be a welcome change. Even if you don't like fish sauce, don't be deterred – all that's left of that fishy, pungent taste after roasting is a thick, caramelised glaze that's full of flavour.

SERVES: 4

PREP: 10 MINUTES / **COOK:** 50 MINUTES / **REST:** 10 MINUTES

1.75kg free-range chicken
1 red onion, peeled and chopped into eighths

MARINADE
⅓ cup (80ml) fish sauce
1 whole coriander plant (i.e. everything attached
    to a single root), root, stems and leaves roughly
    chopped, some leaves reserved for garnish
1 clove garlic, peeled and sliced
2 tbsp caster sugar
3 bird's-eye chillies, thinly sliced
Juice of ½ lemon

Heat the oven to 180°C (fan-forced). Mix together the marinade ingredients, stirring well to dissolve the sugar. Set aside while you prepare the chicken.

Rinse the chicken under running water and pat it dry inside and out with kitchen paper. With kitchen scissors or a heavy knife, cut down either side of the backbone and remove the backbone completely. Remove the wishbone if you like, as this will make carving the breast easier when the chicken is cooked. Press down on the breast of the chicken to flatten it. (Instead of discarding the backbone, if you prefer, chop it into large pieces and place the pieces in the roasting tray to add more flavour to the pan juices.)

Work your fingers under the skin of the breast and thighs of the chicken and spoon the marinade both under and over the skin, as well as on the underside of the chicken. Place the onion pieces in a roasting tray and lay the chicken, skin-side up, on top of the onion.

Roast for 45 minutes, basting every 15 minutes. Remove the chicken when the skin is dark and caramelised (it will be darker than a normal roast chicken from the caramelised sugars in the marinade) and the meat is only just cooked through. Rest the chicken in a warm, draught-free place for at least 10 minutes.

While the chicken is resting, pour the juices from the pan into a jug, leaving the onions in the tray. Skim off any liquid fat, then return to the roasting pan with the onions and place the pan over medium heat. Stir the pan juices and the onions, scraping off any bits stuck to the bottom of the pan. Spoon the sauce and onions over the chicken, scatter with the reserved coriander leaves, and serve.

TIP
Butterflying a chicken in this way is a great mid-week solution to saving time. It only takes a minute or so to do but can shave more than ½ an hour off the cooking time.

BROWN RICE CONGEE WITH CRAB

Congee is a simple, elegant rice porridge that is easy to make. It's a great breakfast, a perfect weapon to combat winter flu, and almost magical in the way just a cup of rice can grow to feed a family. In this version I've included fried Chinese buns rather than the more traditional youtiao croutons, both of which you might want to avoid if you're after a healthier option.

SERVES: 4–6
PREP: 10 MINUTES / **COOK:** 2 HOURS

½ cup brown rice
½ cup white rice
2 litres White Chicken Stock (page 20),
     seafood stock or water
½ tsp salt
200g picked crab meat
Sliced spring onions, to serve
A handful of coriander leaves, to serve
Fresh ginger, sliced into thin strips, to serve
Sliced red chillies, to serve (optional)
Soy sauce, to serve

FRIED MANTOU (OPTIONAL)
2 unfilled Chinese steamed buns (mantou)
     (available from Asian grocers)
Vegetable oil for deep-frying

ONION OIL (OPTIONAL)
3 tbsp peanut oil
½ brown onion, peeled and finely diced
1 clove garlic, peeled and finely chopped
A pinch of salt

Combine the brown and white rice, wash the rice under running water and drain well. Place in a large, heavy-based saucepan along with the stock and salt and bring to a low simmer. Simmer, covered, for 2 hours, stirring occasionally but particularly in the final hour, as it may catch on the bottom of the saucepan.

In the last 10 minutes of cooking, stir through the crab meat. Season to taste, scatter with the spring onion, coriander, ginger and sliced chillies (if using), and drizzle with a little soy sauce to serve.

To make the fried mantou: Cut the steamed buns into 2cm square croutons and fry in very hot oil (200°C) until golden brown. Drain and serve with the congee.

To make the onion oil: Heat 1 tbsp of the oil in a small frypan and fry the onion, garlic and salt for 5 minutes over high heat, until the onion turns golden brown. Add the remaining oil and reduce the heat to low for a further 5 minutes. Allow to cool, then serve with the congee.

TIP
Instead of the crab meat, try stirring through some shredded chicken, flaked white fish, pork mince or any leftover wonton filling, moulded into balls (see page 214).

SANG CHOY BAO

A favourite in Chinese restaurants in both Hong Kong and Australia, 'sang choy bao' means 'lettuce parcels' in Cantonese. It's simple, healthy and makes a great mid-week meal. The mixture also freezes well, so you can make extra and keep it for later.

SERVES: 4
PREP: 15 MINUTES / **STEEP:** 20 MINUTES / **COOK:** 5 MINUTES

4 dried shiitake mushrooms
1 head of iceberg lettuce
500g pork mince
1 tbsp Shaoxing wine
1 tsp light soy sauce
2 tsp cornflour
A pinch of white pepper
2 cloves garlic, peeled and finely chopped
1 tbsp peanut oil, or other vegetable oil
2 spring onions, white and light green parts, trimmed and cut into 1cm lengths
12 green beans (about 75g), cut into 1cm lengths
1 carrot, diced
2 tbsp oyster sauce
1 tsp Cheong Chan caramel sauce, or dark soy sauce
2 tbsp hoisin sauce

Steep the mushrooms in hot water for 20 minutes, then remove from the liquid (reserving the liquid), discard the stems and dice the caps.

Cut the root out of the lettuce and carefully separate the leaves without tearing them. Wash under cold running water and hold in a large bowl or sink full of cold water until ready to use. Trimming any ragged ends off the lettuce leaves will help them keep their cup shapes.

Mix the pork mince with the Shaoxing wine, soy sauce, cornflour, pepper and garlic. Heat a wok until very hot and add the oil. Add the pork mixture and stir-fry until lightly browned, then add the spring onions, beans, carrot and diced mushroom. Stir-fry for about a minute, then add the oyster sauce and caramel sauce (or dark soy sauce). Continue to stir-fry for another 2–3 minutes, or until the meat is cooked through and the vegetables are tender. If the mixture is looking too dry you can add a few tablespoons of the shiitake steeping liquid during cooking. Transfer the mixture to a bowl for serving.

For the sauce, mix together the hoisin sauce and 2 tbsp of the shiitake steeping liquid, and transfer to a small bowl for serving.

Serve the filling and sauce with the lettuce leaves. To assemble the sang choy bao, spoon some filling into a lettuce cup and drizzle over a little of the sauce.

TIP

For something different, try this with chicken or turkey mince. Minced duck breast is especially good.

The Thai name for this dish, 'seua rong hai', literally translates to 'crying tiger' - the hot dipping sauce is supposed to bring tears to your eyes. Don't be too scared, however; it's actually not that hot. The ground toasted rice added to this sauce gives it a wonderful texture.

CRYING TIGER

SERVES: 2–4 (OR MORE AS PART OF A SHARED MEAL)
PREP: 10 MINUTES / **STAND:** 1 HOUR
COOK: 10 MINUTES / **REST:** 5 MINUTES

300g sirloin steak
1 tsp light soy sauce
1 tsp fish sauce

CRYING TIGER SAUCE
½ tsp uncooked white rice
1 tbsp lime juice
1 tbsp fish sauce
1 tsp minced shallot
½ tsp chilli powder
¼ tsp caster sugar
1 tsp shredded coriander leaves

Rub the steak with the soy sauce and fish sauce and let stand at room temperature for about an hour.

In a dry frypan, roast the rice by tossing constantly for 2–3 minutes over medium heat, until it is opaque and just starting to brown in spots. Grind to a rough powder in a mortar and pestle. Combine the powder with the remaining sauce ingredients, stirring well to dissolve the sugar, and set aside.

Grill the steak under very high heat, or fry in a heavy frypan, until cooked to your liking. Set aside in a warm place to rest for about half the time it took to cook. Slice the steak thinly and serve on a warmed plate with the sauce in a bowl on the side for dipping.

TIP
If you like it really spicy, add two minced bird's-eye chillies to the sauce for an extra kick. Also, don't limit yourself to beef. This is a great dipping sauce for all kinds of grilled meats.

CARAMELISED LEMONGRASS PORK CHOPS

There is a wonderfully appealing simplicity and balance to Vietnamese food. A simple pork chop marinated in lemongrass and fish sauce can be found on almost every Vietnamese home or restaurant menu, and for good reason – it's just delicious. The nuoc cham sauce is the key to this dish.

SERVES: 4

PREP: 10 MINUTES / **MARINATE:** 30 MINUTES / **COOK:** 10 MINUTES

---

4 boneless pork neck steaks (sometimes called pork Scotch fillet), about 200g each, or 4 pork chops
1 tsp peanut oil, or other vegetable oil
Salt and pepper for seasoning
Cooked rice, to serve
A handful of coriander leaves, to serve
Sliced tomato, to serve
Cucumber, to serve
Pickled Carrot & Daikon (page 30)

LEMONGRASS MARINADE
2 tbsp soft brown sugar
2 cloves garlic, peeled and minced
2 stalks lemongrass, white part only, minced
⅓ cup fish sauce
¼ tsp black pepper
1 tbsp peanut oil, or other vegetable oil

NUOC CHAM SAUCE
1 clove garlic
2 red bird's-eye chillies
Juice of 1 lime (about 50ml)
1 tbsp caster sugar
3 tbsp water
1½ tbsp fish sauce

Place the pork on a chopping board and lightly beat with a meat mallet until about 1cm thin. If using pork chops, carefully beat around the bone.

Mix together all the ingredients for the lemongrass marinade, pour it over the pork and ensure it is well coated. Marinate for at least 30 minutes, or preferably overnight.

For the nuoc cham sauce, pound the garlic and chilli together in a mortar and pestle to a rough paste (alternatively, finely chop together on a chopping board). Mix together the lime juice, sugar and water and taste it, adjusting the sweetness and sourness to taste. Add the fish sauce a little at a time, tasting as you go, until the sauce is savoury but still pleasant, without being overpowered by the fish sauce. Mix through the chilli and garlic paste and set aside until ready to use.

Heat the oil in a frypan over high heat. Season the pork with salt and pepper and fry for about 2–3 minutes each side, or until cooked through. Add a little of the lemongrass marinade a minute or two before you remove the pork to further caramelise in the pan. Rest the pork for 3 minutes in a warm, draught-free place.

Serve the pork with rice (broken rice if you have it), coriander, tomato and cucumber, some Pickled Carrot & Daikon and a little nuoc cham on the side. You can even add a fried egg if you like.

TIP
When trying to find a good balance between the salty, sweet, sour and bitter elements of Asian sauces and dressings, it's easiest to start with balancing the sweet and sour elements first, then gradually add the salty and bitter ones until you have a well-flavoured, savoury sauce. Make extra nuoc cham and keep it in the fridge until ready to use.

CRYSTAL PRAWNS WITH CELERY

Crystal prawns are a Shanghainese speciality. No trip to Shanghai would be complete without a plate of them. The traditional dish serves the prawns just on their own, with vinegar to drizzle, but I prefer the crunch of the celery and the spring onion in this version.

SERVES: 2 (OR MORE AS PART OF A SHARED MEAL)
PREP: 10 MINUTES / **COOK:** 5 MINUTES

12 large raw prawns (about 200g), peeled
   and deveined
1 tbsp cornflour
2 tsp salt
1 tbsp peanut oil, or other vegetable oil
1 stalk celery, thinly sliced on the diagonal
1 spring onion, white and light green parts,
   trimmed and thinly sliced on the diagonal
1 tbsp Chinkiang black vinegar, to serve
   (optional)

SAUCE
½ cup White Chicken Stock (page 20)
½ tsp caster sugar
2 tbsp Shaoxing wine
1 tsp ginger juice, squeezed from 1 tbsp
   grated ginger
A pinch of white pepper
1 tsp cornflour

Place the prawns in a large bowl, sprinkle over the cornflour and rub it into the prawns for about a minute. Rinse under running water. Return the prawns to the bowl, sprinkle over the salt and repeat the rubbing and rinsing process. Drain well.

Combine the sauce ingredients, stirring to make sure the cornflour doesn't settle at the bottom. Add the oil to a hot wok and then add the prawns. Stir-fry for about a minute, or until they start to turn opaque. Add the celery and spring onion to the wok and toss for about a minute, or until they soften.

Pour over the sauce and cook for a further 2 minutes, or until the sauce bubbles and thickens, then transfer to a plate and serve with the Chinkiang black vinegar on the side, if you like. Drizzle a little vinegar over the prawns when you eat them.

TIP
Rubbing with salt and cornflour not only seasons the prawns, it also keeps them looking white in the cooking process.

FRESH HERB & PRAWN SALAD

This is a simple, delicious mid-week salad that contains no oil. Mixing and balancing the dressing is a matter of taste, because limes vary in their sourness and different brands of fish sauce have a different pungency. Follow the method in this recipe, trust your tastebuds and you'll have a perfect dressing every time.

SERVES: 2 (OR MORE AS PART OF A SHARED MEAL)
PREP: 15 MINUTES / **COOK:** 5 MINUTES

1 bunch coriander, leaves picked
1 bunch mint, leaves picked
1 carrot, cut into thin matchsticks
1 continental cucumber, cut into thin matchsticks
1 red onion, peeled and thinly sliced
3 leaves Chinese cabbage, shredded (optional)
12 large raw prawns, peeled and deveined, tails on
A pinch of salt

DRESSING
Juice of 2 limes (about 50ml)
1½ tsp palm sugar or caster sugar, or to taste
1 tbsp fish sauce
1 bird's-eye chilli, sliced
½ tsp grated ginger

For the dressing, mix together the lime juice and sugar until the sugar is dissolved, tasting to ensure the sourness of the lime is balanced by the sweetness of the sugar. It should taste nice; as if you could drink it. Add the fish sauce a little at a time until the dressing becomes pleasantly savoury without being overpoweringly fishy. Mix through the chilli and grated ginger and allow the dressing to stand in the fridge until ready to serve.

Mix together the salad ingredients. Split the prawns in two from the head to the tail, leaving the tail intact. Bring a saucepan of water to the boil and add salt as if for boiling pasta. Drop in the prawns and stir just until they turn opaque. Remove from the water and drain well. The prawns will continue to cook a little out of the water, but rather than refreshing them in iced water, I prefer to add them to the salad while warm.

Toss the prawns and the dressing through the mixed salad. Serve immediately.

TIP
You can also add a little shredded chicken breast to this salad. For instructions on steaming chicken breast, have a look at the Bang-Bang Chicken Salad recipe (page 58).

CHICKEN FAT NOODLES

While the idea of noodles fried in chicken fat may sound like a heart attack waiting to happen, they are actually no more oily than other fried noodles. Using the liquid fat, crispy scratchings and thigh meat, these simple fried noodles have very few seasonings, bringing out just the pure taste of the bird. This is definitely one for chicken lovers. Maybe don't eat it every day.

SERVES: 4

PREP: 20 MINUTES / **RENDER:** 2 HOURS / **COOK:** 15 MINUTES

2 tbsp chicken fat (trimmed from a whole chicken or chicken thighs), roughly chopped, or 2 tbsp peanut oil
400g chicken thighs, skinless, sliced thinly across the grain
1kg Hokkien noodles
5 cloves garlic, peeled and roughly chopped
1 tsp sea salt
A pinch of caster sugar
3 tbsp dark soy sauce
¼ tsp white pepper
¼ cup White Chicken Stock (page 20), or water
200g beansprouts
5–6 spring onions, trimmed and sliced
Lemon or lime wedges, to serve
Sliced chillies and soy sauce, to serve (optional)
Pickled Carrot & Daikon (page 30), to serve (optional)

MARINADE

2 tsp Shaoxing wine
2 tsp sesame oil
2 tsp dark soy sauce
2 tsp cornflour

Heat the oven to 100°C. Render the fat from the trimmed chicken fat by placing in an ovenproof pan and baking for 2 hours. Pour off and set aside the liquid fat, and reserve any crispy 'scratchings' that remain in the pan. (You may want to increase the heat towards the end of the rendering time to crisp the scratchings if they are still soft.)

Mix together the marinade ingredients in a bowl and add the chicken. Tease apart the noodles so that they separate. If you have trouble separating them, soak in a large bowl of warm water.

Heat a wok until smoking and add 2 tbsp of the rendered chicken fat. Fry the garlic until starting to brown, then add the chicken and its marinade. Add the salt and sugar and toss to coat. Fry for about 2–3 minutes, until the chicken is nearly cooked through. Add the noodles, soy sauce, white pepper and White Chicken Stock. Stir-fry for 3–4 minutes, or until the noodles start to soften. Use a pair of strong tongs to toss the noodles.

When the noodles are just starting to soften, toss through the beansprouts and remove from the heat. Off the heat, toss through the spring onion and reserved scratchings. Serve immediately with wedges of lemon or lime and, if you like, some chillies in a little soy sauce and the Pickled Carrot & Daikon.

TIP

If you prefer more vegetables than just the beansprouts and spring onions, you can add carrot matchsticks, bok choy or any other vegetables you like.

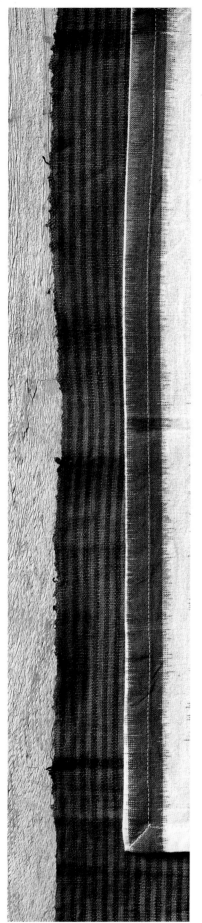

A 'donburi' is a Japanese rice bowl; it's also the name given to an endless number of one-bowl dishes that are perfect mid-week meals. This salmon and avocado version is simple and delicious, with a bit of indulgence in the form of dressed salmon roe.

SALMON & AVOCADO DONBURI

SERVES: 4
PREP: 10 MINUTES / **COOK:** 10 MINUTES

3–4 small salmon fillets, about 150g each
2 tsp peanut oil, or other vegetable oil
Salt, to taste
6 cups cooked short-grain rice, to serve
2 avocados, sliced
2 tbsp salmon roe
1 tbsp Umami Sauce (page 29), or light soy sauce
1 nori sheet, thinly sliced, to serve (optional)
Wasabi, to serve

Using a sharp knife, score the skin side of the salmon at ½cm intervals along its length, cutting through the skin but not through the flesh. Heat a large frypan until very hot and add 1 tsp of the oil. Season the skin side of two of the salmon fillets with a little salt, and fry, skin-side down, for 3 minutes. Flip and fry for a further 2 minutes. Set aside on a rack to rest for about 3 minutes.

Divide the cooked rice between four bowls and top with the sliced avocado. Break up the salmon with two spoons and scatter over the avocado. Mix together the salmon roe and Umami Sauce and spoon over the salmon. Scatter with a little nori (if using), add some wasabi on the side of the bowl, and serve.

TIP
When frying fish, the pan needs to be very hot or the skin may stick to the pan. If you'd prefer not to fry the fish, you can bake it and discard the skin, as shown on page 195.

Across most of South-East Asia the streets are lined with shops selling all kinds of delicacies. I remember travelling around Malaysia a lot with my family when I was young and being dazzled by the array of foods just a few steps from our car door – fresh rambutans, steaming bowls of noodles, roasted ducks and fried chicken. One of my favourite stops would always be the man selling deep-fried bananas. This is more than a banana fritter; it's a part of my childhood.

MALAYSIAN DEEP-FRIED BANANAS (GORENG PISANG)

SERVES: 4

PREP: 10 MINUTES / **COOK:** 10 MINUTES

1 cup self-raising flour
1 tbsp cornflour
2 tsp baking powder
A pinch of salt
200ml ice-cold water
4 ripe bananas, peeled
Vegetable oil for deep-frying (about 2 litres)

Sieve the dry ingredients together into a large bowl and lightly whisk through the cold water. Take care not to over-mix the batter; a few lumps are fine.

Heat the oil to 170°C in a wok. Dip the bananas into the batter then slide them into the oil. Deep-fry for 8–10 minutes, until the batter is golden brown and crispy. Remove the bananas from the oil and drain well. Serve with Simplest Coconut Ice Cream (page 146), or just as they are.

TIP

The carbon dioxide given off from the baking powder and self-raising flour bubbles through the batter as it cooks giving you a deliciously light and crispy batter.

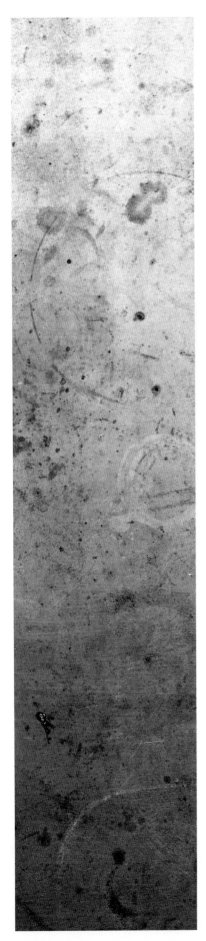
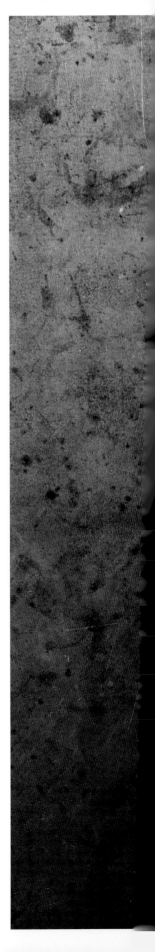

Simplicity is so important in home cooking, and I love this recipe because you get fantastic results that far outweigh the effort. If you have an ice cream machine, I hope this becomes a go-to recipe for you as it has for me.

SIMPLEST COCONUT ICE CREAM

MAKES: ABOUT 700 MILLILITRES OF ICE CREAM
PREP: 5 MINUTES / **COOK:** 5 MINUTES / **FREEZE:** 2 HOURS

1 can (400ml) coconut milk
1 tub (300ml) thickened cream
½ cup caster sugar
Fresh cut fruits and mint leaves, to serve

Place the coconut milk, cream and sugar in a saucepan and bring to a simmer. Watch the mixture carefully to ensure it doesn't boil over. Stir well and simmer for 5 minutes.

Chill, and then churn in an ice cream maker in accordance with the manufacturer's instructions. Chill the ice cream in the freezer for at least 2 hours. Serve the ice cream with fresh tropical fruits and scatter with a little chopped mint leaves.

TIP

For a quick, impressive dinner party dessert, match this ice cream with some fresh or tinned lychees and some large mint leaves that have been deep fried for just a few seconds until they are crispy and translucent green.

THURSDAY

Some versions of this simple salad call for the vegetables to be roughly diced, but I find the finely chopped version gives a more delicate texture. I eat this most often with Japanese curry (try it with the recipe on page 169, for example), but it is a great accompaniment for Mexican, Indian or African dishes, grilled meats or anything with a bit of spice.

KACHUMBER

SERVE: AS PART OF A SHARED MEAL
PREP: 10 MINUTES / **STAND:** 10 MINUTES

1 continental cucumber or 2 Lebanese cucumbers,
  peeled and deseeded
3 Roma tomatoes, peeled and deseeded
½ red onion, peeled
1 bird's-eye chilli, thinly sliced
1 tbsp chopped coriander leaves
1 tbsp finely chopped mint leaves
Juice of ½ lime
¼ tsp ground cumin
¼ tsp salt flakes
A pinch of caster sugar

Cut the cucumber, tomato and onion into a 5mm-square dice and combine in a large bowl. Add the chilli, coriander and mint to the bowl and mix together. Add the remaining ingredients, mix well and let stand for 10 minutes before serving.

TIP
Try this as a salsa on top of some simple baked salmon.

WINTER PORK & MISO SOUP (TONJIRU)

The first time I tried this soup - called tonjiru in Japanese - was one night in Tokyo, visiting a beautiful winter garden with a few friends. It was probably only about 2 or 3 degrees Celsius, and there was frost on the ground, but this soup kept us all warm and happy. What I love about it is that it's quick to make, but gives you the feeling of something that's been lovingly cooked for hours. It's been a cold-weather favourite of mine ever since I first tried it.

SERVES: 4
PREP: 15 MINUTES / **COOK:** 25 MINUTES

1 kg piece pork belly, skin and bone removed
2 litres White Chicken Stock (page 20), or dashi stock, or vegetable stock
1 small brown onion, peeled and thickly sliced
2 carrots, peeled and cut into irregular chunks
1 orange-fleshed sweet potato, peeled and cut into irregular chunks
150g shimeji mushrooms
½ large daikon (white radish), quartered lengthways and cut into 1cm slices
2 tsp salt
2 tbsp sake
½ tsp sugar
2 tbsp mirin
1 block (300g) silken tofu, cut into 2cm cubes (optional)
¼ cup white miso
2 spring onions, trimmed and thinly sliced, to serve

Cut the pork belly into 3cm strips and then into 1cm slices.

Heat a large saucepan and add the pork belly and a tablespoon or two of the White Chicken Stock. (The stock will stop the pork belly from sticking until the fat starts to render.) Alternatively, you can use 1 tsp of vegetable oil. Fry the pork until it begins to brown, then add the onion, carrot, sweet potato, mushrooms and daikon and continue to fry for a minute or two. Add the remaining stock, salt, sake, sugar and mirin and simmer for 20 minutes, or until the vegetables are tender, skimming off any scum that rises to the surface. Add the tofu, if using, and warm through.

Place the miso in a large ladle. Scoop a little of the soup into the ladle and stir to dissolve the miso to a thick liquid. Stir this liquid through the soup and remove from the heat. (Don't bring it to the boil again, as it will spoil the flavour of the miso.)

Scatter with spring onion and serve.

TIP
Some more traditional inclusions to this soup are gobo (burdock root) and konyakku (devil's tongue jelly). Both are available from Japanese grocers, so give them a try.

FILLET STEAK WITH RED MISO BUTTER

One of the easiest ways to add flavour to meats or vegetables is with flavoured butters. It takes just a few minutes to make a big batch that will last in the freezer for months, always ready to add a punch of flavour. The proportions for the butter in this recipe make much more than you will need for four serves, but you won't regret having extra to keep.

SERVES: 4
PREP: 15 MINUTES / **COOK:** VARIABLE

4 thick fillet steaks (about 200g each)
Olive oil and sea salt, to taste

RED MISO BUTTER
500g unsalted butter, softened
200g red miso (or white miso)
1 tbsp light soy sauce
1 bunch (about 20g) chives, finely chopped

To make the red miso butter, place the softened butter in the bowl of a stand mixer and whip for about 10 minutes, or until it is very pale. Add the miso and soy sauce and beat until well combined, then fold through the chives. Divide the mixture into half and roll in cling film into long cylinders just a little smaller in diameter than your steaks. Put in the fridge or freezer to firm until ready to use.

Heat a heavy-based frypan until very hot, brush the steaks with a little olive oil and season well with salt. Cook the steaks to your liking (cooking time will vary with the thickness of the steaks), then rest in a warm, draught-free place for half the time the steaks took to cook.

Cut thick rounds from your cylinder of butter and place one on top of each steak. Gratiné with a blowtorch or under a very hot overhead grill until the butter starts to brown. Serve immediately.

TIP
Try spreading this butter over the skin of a chicken for roasting, or over thick wedges of parboiled cabbage, roasted with the butter until blackened and crisp on the edges.

A simple dish of vegetables in oyster sauce should be a part of any cook's repertoire. Like all vegetables, watch that you don't overcook Asian greens, as they are best with a bit of crunch. Instead of pak choy, you could use gai lan, choy sum, bok choy or any other green vegetable.

PAK CHOY WITH OYSTER SAUCE

SERVE: AS PART OF A SHARED MEAL
PREP: 5 MINUTES / **COOK:** 5 MINUTES

4 pak choy
2 tbsp peanut oil, or other vegetable oil
2 thick slices ginger, bruised
2 cloves garlic, peeled and roughly chopped
A pinch of salt

SAUCE
1 tbsp oyster sauce
1 tsp cornflour
½ cup White Chicken Stock (page 20)

Trim any tough root base from the pak choy and slice lengthways into quarters. Wash well under cold running water, then soak in water until ready to use. Mix together the sauce ingredients.

Heat a wok over high heat and pour the oil around the edges. Add the ginger and fry for a few seconds, then add the garlic and salt and continue to fry until the garlic starts to brown. Add the pak choy and toss to coat in the oil, garlic and ginger. Toss for a few more minutes until the pak choy starts to soften, then pour in the sauce. Cover and simmer for a minute or two, or until the sauce thickens and the pak choy is tender. Remove the ginger slices, transfer to a plate and serve.

TIP
If you don't want to use oyster sauce, try a simple garlic sauce by adding in a few extra cloves of chopped garlic and replacing the oyster sauce with ¼ tsp salt and ¼ tsp sugar.

CHICKEN KRA-POW

Kra-pow is the popular Thai holy basil stir-fry. If you can't find holy basil, Thai basil or ordinary sweet basil can easily be substituted (although technically the name would be different, as kra-pow refers to the holy basil). For a hotter version, add a few bird's-eye chillies into the mix.

SERVES: 2–3 (OR MORE AS PART OF A SHARED MEAL)
PREP: 10 MINUTES / **COOK:** 5 MINUTES

3 cloves garlic, peeled
2 large red chillies, deseeded
2 skinless chicken thighs and one skinless breast, roughly minced, or 500g chicken mince
1 tbsp oyster sauce
2 tbsp peanut oil, or other vegetable oil
2 tbsp fish sauce
½ tsp caster sugar
1½ cups loosely packed torn holy basil leaves, or Thai or sweet basil
Fried eggs, to serve (optional)
Lime wedges and cooked rice, to serve

Roughly chop the garlic and chilli together on a board. In a separate bowl, mix together the chicken and oyster sauce.

Heat a wok over high heat and add the oil. Fry the garlic and chilli for a few minutes until fragrant, then add the chicken. Toss in the wok for a minute or so, then add the fish sauce and sugar. Continue to stir-fry for another minute or so, moistening with a little water or stock if it starts to get too dry.

Stir through the basil leaves and remove to a plate. Top with a soft-yolk fried egg, if you like, and serve with a wedge of lime and some rice.

TIP

Try this with beef, pork or turkey mince, or even with sliced squid for something different. You can also substitute an extra tablespoon of fish sauce if you don't have any oyster sauce.

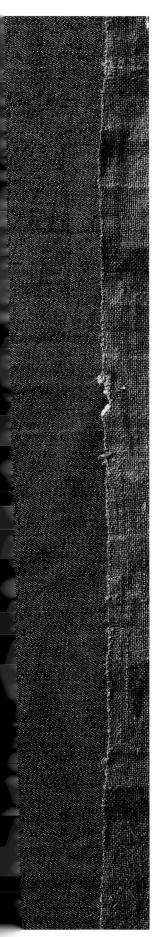
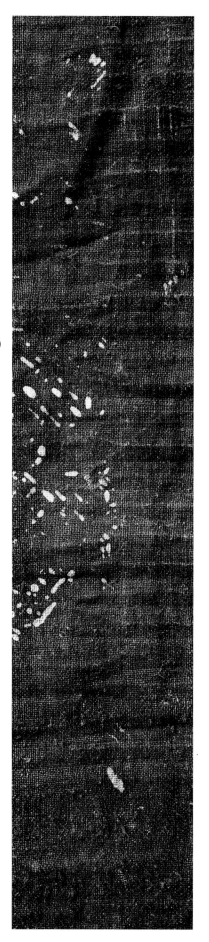

Now we pull back the curtain on just how simple it is to create delicious Asian food with a little bit of forward planning. If you've been sceptical about the benefits of a good master stock, let this dish dispel all doubt.

MASTER STOCK FRIED CHICKEN & FIVE-SPICE SALT

SERVES: 4

COOK: 30 MINUTES / **REST:** 15 MINUTES

Faster Master (page 28) or other master stock (about 2 litres)
4 chicken marylands, skin on
Vegetable oil for deep-frying (about 2 litres)
Cooked rice and Asian greens, to serve

FIVE-SPICE SALT

2 tbsp salt flakes
¼ tsp Chinese five-spice powder
A pinch of ground black pepper

For the five-spice salt, place the salt in a frypan and dry-fry for 2–3 minutes, or until very dry and granular. Mix with the five-spice powder and pepper and use a mortar and pestle to grind to a powder. Set aside until ready to serve.

Bring the Faster Master to a low boil in a large saucepan. Watch it carefully, as it is prone to boiling over. Add the chicken marylands, skin-side down, and simmer, covered, over very low heat for 10 minutes. Turn off the heat and leave the chicken in the liquid, still covered, for 15 minutes. Remove the chicken from the liquid carefully so as not to damage the skin. Drain and rest, uncovered, on a wire rack for a further 15 minutes.

Heat the oil for deep-frying to 190°C in a deep-fryer, wok or wide saucepan. Gently pat the chicken dry all over with kitchen paper and deep-fry for 2 minutes, or until the skin is crisp. Drain again and serve with rice, Asian greens and some five-spice salt on the side.

TIP
Try this with jointed chicken wings for a quick snack or to feed a crowd.

MUSHROOM RICE

This flavourful rice would be a great side dish for grilled salmon, which is a traditional autumnal fish in Japan. Or for a simple meal in itself, just team this with some Asazuke (page 77) and a bowl of good miso soup.

SERVES: 4
PREP: 10 MINUTES / **COOK:** 30 MINUTES / **STAND:** 2 MINUTES

250g mixed fresh Asian mushrooms, such as shiitake, enoki, shimeji or King oyster (eringi)
1 tbsp peanut oil, or other vegetable oil
2 cloves garlic, peeled and minced
3 spring onions, white and light green parts, trimmed and sliced diagonally
1 tsp sea salt
440g uncooked short-grain rice
750ml White Chicken Stock (page 20), or water, or vegetable stock
3 tbsp light soy sauce
2 tbsp sake
1 tbsp mirin

Slice or tear the mushrooms into bite-sized pieces. Heat the oil in a large, heavy-based saucepan over high heat, add the garlic, mushrooms, spring onion and salt and sauté until the mushrooms start to soften. Add the rice and mix through.

Add the stock, soy sauce, sake and mirin and bring to the boil. Continue to boil for 5 minutes, uncovered, until the water level reduces to the top of the rice mixture. Cover tightly and reduce the heat to very low for 15 minutes. Turn off the heat and leave the rice standing, covered, for a further 5 minutes.

Remove the lid and stir the rice with a cutting motion, leaving it uncovered for a further 2 minutes to fluff the rice and drive off excess moisture.

TIP

For a stronger mushroom flavour, use dried shiitake mushrooms instead of fresh ones and soak them in 2 cups of hot water for 20 minutes. Remove the stems and slice the mushrooms, using the reserved soaking liquid in place of some of the stock for cooking the rice.

NAGOYA-STYLE CHICKEN WINGS

The recipe for these wings originated in Nagoya but they are now a favourite at many casual restaurants (izakayas) around Japan. The black pepper together with the sweet soy glaze is a magnificent combination, and you'd never think that something so delicious could be so simple to make.

SERVES: 4 (OR AS PART OF A SHARED MEAL)
PREP: 10 MINUTES / **COOK:** 20 MINUTES

1½ kg chicken wings (about 12–15 wings)
2 cups Light Teriyaki (page 32)
1 tbsp caster sugar
½ cup cornflour
Vegetable oil for deep-frying (about 2 litres)
Freshly ground black pepper, to serve
Toasted sesame seeds, to serve

To prepare the chicken wings, cut through the second joint from the wingtip, separating each wing into the drumette and the wingette/wing tip. You only need the wingette side for this recipe, but of course you can treat the drumette in the same way, or just reserve it for a different purpose. Cutting the wings like this ensures they sit completely covered by the teriyaki sauce. If using the drumettes as well, make sure you have extra cornflour to coat them. You do not need to increase the quantities of the glaze.

Heat the Light Teriyaki and caster sugar in a saucepan, stirring until the sugar is dissolved, then simmer for 5 minutes, uncovered, to reduce slightly in volume. Meanwhile, toss the chicken wings in the cornflour to coat well, and set aside for 5 minutes, uncovered, before frying.

Heat the oil to 160°C in a deep-fryer, wok or wide saucepan and deep-fry the wings in batches for about 5 minutes each, or until browned and cooked through. Remove the wings from the oil and plunge straight into the warm teriyaki glaze until they are well coated, then transfer to a wire rack to dry. Repeat for the remaining chicken.

To serve, grind over plenty of black pepper (the more the better) and scatter some toasted sesame seeds on top.

TIP

This technique of plunging deep-fried foods straight into a seasoning liquid is common in Japanese cuisine. Although it may seem strange to lose some of the crunch of deep-frying, you gain a silky surface texture with lots of flavour.

BEEF BULGOGI

Bulgogi is a common Korean dish. The sweet and smoky grilled beef goes perfectly with rice, tangy kimchi and fresh lettuce leaves. You can thinly slice any of a number of different tender cuts of beef for this dish, or you can buy pre-sliced beef from Asian grocers and butchers.

SERVES: 4

PREP: 15 MINUTES / **CHILL:** 2 HOURS / **MARINATE:** 1 HOUR / **COOK:** 10 MINUTES

1kg beef, Scotch fillet, rump or topside
2 tsp toasted sesame seeds
2 tbsp peanut oil, or other vegetable oil
Cooked rice, to serve
Kimchi, to serve
Butter lettuce leaves, to serve

MARINADE
1 small brown onion, peeled and roughly chopped
1 nashi pear, peeled and cored
6 cloves garlic, peeled
½ cup soy sauce
2 tbsp caster sugar
2 tbsp honey
1 tbsp sesame oil
¼ cup cold water (or sake, if you prefer)

Chill the beef in the freezer for 2 hours then slice thinly across the grain.

Combine the marinade ingredients in a food processor and process to a purée. Place the beef in a Ziploc bag, add the marinade and knead the bag to rub marinade into the beef. Marinate for at least 1 hour, or preferably overnight. If you prefer, the marinated beef can be frozen at this stage and thawed for use later.

Heat the oil on a large hot barbecue hotplate or large frypan and cook the beef. Do this in batches if you need to. Scatter with toasted sesame seeds.

Serve the bulgogi with rice, a little kimchi and butter lettuce leaves. Put a little rice, bulgogi and kimchi into a lettuce leaf, wrap it up and pop it into your mouth.

TIP
You can make a spicy bulgogi by adding a teaspoon of Korean chilli powder and a few bird's-eye chillies to the marinade. Any leftover bulgogi can be used to make Bibimbap (page 178).

JAPANESE BEEF CURRY

Japanese curry is different from the dishes of the Indian subcontinent in that it is created from a European-style roux, richly flavoured into a thick curry sauce used to coat the main ingredients. Although traditionally served with Japanese pickles such as rakkyo and fukujinzuke, these can be hard to find. Try Kachumber (page 150) instead for the perfect fresh accompaniment.

SERVES: 4

PREP: 20 MINUTES / **COOK:** 2 HOURS / **STAND:** 15 MINUTES

1 kg chuck steak, cut into large cubes

Salt and pepper, to taste

1 tbsp peanut oil, or other vegetable oil

1.5 litres White Chicken Stock (page 20), or beef stock, or water

2 Sebago potatoes, peeled and cut into irregular chunks

2 large carrots, peeled and cut into irregular chunks

60g unsalted butter

80g plain flour

2 tbsp curry powder

1 tbsp garam masala

¼ tsp chilli powder (or to taste)

1 large brown onion, peeled and thickly sliced

2 tbsp tomato sauce

1 tsp Worcestershire sauce

1 tbsp soy sauce

½ apple, peeled and grated

Cooked rice, to serve

Kachumber (page 150), to serve

Season the steak with salt and pepper. Heat the oil in a large saucepan and fry the beef in batches until well browned. Set aside. Deglaze the saucepan with the stock and bring to a simmer. Add the beef and simmer for 1–1½ hours or until the beef is tender when pierced with a fork, skimming to remove any scum that forms on the surface. Add the potato and carrot and simmer for a further 15 minutes, or until the vegetables are tender. Remove from the heat, strain out the solids and reserve the stock.

Heat another large saucepan over medium heat and add the butter and flour. Stir with a wooden spoon to combine into a roux, and cook until just starting to turn colour. Add the curry powder, garam masala and chilli powder and stir for 1 minute. Add the reserved stock, a ladleful at a time, until a smooth sauce develops. You can add more stock or water if it is too thick. Add the onion, tomato sauce, Worcestershire sauce, soy sauce and grated apple and simmer for 10 minutes, or until the onion is softened, stirring regularly to stop the sauce from sticking to the bottom of the saucepan. Remove from the heat.

Stir through the beef, potatoes and carrot, season to taste (you will probably need to add some salt) and allow to stand, covered, for at least 15 minutes before serving. Serve with rice and Kachumber.

TIP

This version uses beef, but you could easily substitute any other meat or vegetable you like. For another Japanese favourite, katsu kare, make the sauce only and use that as a topping for a crumbed and fried pork cutlet.

BEEF KOROKKE WITH MISO–MUSTARD MAYONNAISE

'Korokke' is the Japanese term for croquettes, and these basic beef numbers are made a little bit special by the addition of a salty and umami-packed dipping mayonnaise.

MAKES: 8 CROQUETTES
PREP: 30 MINUTES / **COOK:** 30 MINUTES

6 large sebago potatoes, peeled and cut into
    large chunks
1 tsp peanut oil, or other vegetable oil
½ brown onion, peeled and finely diced
200g beef mince
½ tsp sea salt
¼ tsp white pepper
1 cup flour
2 eggs, beaten
2 cups Japanese panko breadcrumbs
Vegetable oil, for deep-frying (about 2 litres)

MISO–MUSTARD MAYONNAISE

1 tbsp white miso
1 tsp hot English mustard
½ cup mayonnaise (preferably Japanese)

Boil the potatoes in plenty of salted water until tender when tested with a knife or skewer (about 10–15 minutes). Drain well then return to the dry saucepan on low heat for a minute or two, tossing regularly to remove any excess moisture. Mash the potatoes or push them through a drum sieve, and set aside.

Heat the oil in a frypan over high heat and fry the onion for a few minutes, until it is soft and transparent. Add the beef, season with salt and fry for 3–4 minutes, or until well browned. Tip out onto kitchen paper to remove as much oil as possible. Transfer the meat and onion mixture to a bowl, add the mashed potato and pepper and mix until well combined.

Form the mixture into eight flat, oval-shaped croquettes approximately 10cm long and 3cm thick. Arrange three plates with flour in one, egg in the second, and panko breadcrumbs in the third. Dip each croquette into flour, then egg and lastly into the breadcrumbs, ensuring that they are completely covered.

Heat the vegetable oil to 180°C in a deep-fryer, wok or wide saucepan. Deep-fry the croquettes for 2–3 minutes, or until golden brown. Remove and drain on a wire rack.

For the miso-mustard mayonnaise, mix all mayonnaise ingredients together until completely combined. Serve the croquettes with the miso-mustard mayonnaise on the side.

TIP

For a variation, you could flavour the beef mince with a little curry powder and replace half of the potato with sweet potato.

BBQ GENGHIS KHAN

Despite the name, this is not actually a Mongolian recipe. Genghis Khan (or Jingisukan) is a popular grilled lamb dish in Hokkaido, Japan's northernmost island, and is so named for the curved hotplate on which it is commonly cooked, said to resemble a Mongolian shield. This version does away with the need for any special hotplates, and is perfect for a mid-week barbecue.

SERVES: 4–6

PREP: 30 MINUTES / **MARINATE:** OVERNIGHT / **COOK:** 15 MINUTES

1.5kg lamb leg or forequarter chops, deboned and sliced on an angle into large pieces (you can use whole chops if you prefer)
1 tbsp peanut oil, or other vegetable oil
¼ Japanese pumpkin (such as the Kent variety), peeled and cut into thin wedges
¼ head of cabbage, separated into leaves
1 green capsicum, deseeded and sliced
125g beansprouts, rinsed and drained
1 brown onion, peeled and cut into rings

GENGHIS KHAN SAUCE

125ml sake
60ml mirin
200ml light soy sauce
50ml dark soy sauce
2 apples, peeled and cored
1 white peach, peeled and stoned
1 brown onion, peeled and roughly chopped
2 thick slices ginger (about 15g), peeled
3 cloves garlic, peeled
1 tsp chilli powder
¼ tsp ground black pepper
3 tbsp caster sugar
A pinch of ground cinnamon

For the Genghis Khan sauce, place all the ingredients in a food processor or blender and process to a relatively smooth purée. Pour about one-third of the sauce over the lamb and marinate in the fridge overnight. Keep the rest of the sauce in the fridge overnight before using, as it needs time for the flavours to develop.

Heat your barbecue hotplate or grill until very hot and brush with oil. Put a little of everything onto the barbecue and cook until done to your liking, removing each vegetable once cooked and placing on a warmed serving plate. When the vegetables are cooked and on the serving plate, top with the cooked lamb. As the lamb rests, the juices will run down and flavour the vegetables. Serve with the remaining Genghis Khan sauce (brought to room temperature) for dipping both the meat and the vegetables in.

TIP

The Genghis Khan sauce can be used as a marinade or dipping sauce, or both. I prefer to use it as both.

For many weeknight meals, desserts don't need to be any more complicated than a single scoop of good ice cream. The first time I had a scoop of sesame and honey ice cream was in a Japanese restaurant more than 20 years ago. I still remember it as the perfect end to a great meal.

SESAME & HONEY ICE CREAM

MAKES: ABOUT 1 LITRE OF ICE CREAM
PREP: 15 MINUTES / **COOK:** 10 MINUTES / **FREEZE:** 3 HOURS

4 tbsp (60g) white sesame seeds
3 tbsp tahini
300ml pouring cream
400ml full-cream milk
⅓ cup honey
6 egg yolks
⅓ cup (80g) caster sugar

Toast the sesame seeds in a dry frypan over medium heat until golden and fragrant, then grind in a mortar and pestle to a smooth paste. Transfer to a medium saucepan, add the tahini, cream, milk and honey and bring to a simmer.

Whisk the egg yolks and caster sugar in a heatproof bowl until the yolks are pale and slightly lightened. Pour the hot milk mixture over the egg mixture, whisking constantly, then immediately transfer everything back to the saucepan. Heat over low heat, stirring constantly, until the mixture is thick enough to coat the back of a spoon. Chill the mixture well, then churn in an ice cream maker in accordance with the manufacturer's instructions.

Chill the ice cream in the freezer for at least 2 hours before serving.

TIP
For a black sesame ice cream, just use black sesame seeds instead of white, and black sesame paste (available from Japanese grocers), instead of tahini.

FRIDAY

BIBIMBAP

I love simple, one-bowl dishes and bibimbap, from Korea, is one of my favourites. I particularly like the hot stone bowl version for the little bits of crispy rice you get from frying in the bowl, but if you don't have a hot stone bowl, an ordinary bowl version is just as satisfying.

SERVES: 4
PREP: 15 MINUTES / **COOK:** 20 MINUTES

1 zucchini, cut into matchsticks
1 carrot, cut into matchsticks
100g enoki mushrooms
100g fresh shiitake mushrooms, roots removed and sliced
2–3 tbsp sesame oil
Salt, to taste
100g Spicy Beansprout Salad (page 112)
4 eggs
6–8 cups cooked short-grain rice
1 Lebanese cucumber, cut into matchsticks

MINCED BEEF MIX

2 tsp sesame oil
2 cloves garlic, peeled and minced
250g beef mince
1 tbsp light soy sauce
½ tsp caster sugar
Salt, to taste

BIBIMBAP SAUCE

¼ cup water
1 tbsp caster sugar
½ cup Korean chilli-bean paste (gochujang)
2 tbsp sesame oil

First prepare the minced beef mix. Heat the sesame oil in a frypan over medium heat and fry the garlic until starting to brown. Add the beef mince, soy sauce and sugar. Season with a little salt and toss the beef until cooked through.

To prepare the bibimbap sauce, heat the water and caster sugar over medium heat in a small saucepan, stirring until the sugar is dissolved. Remove from the heat and stir in the chilli paste and sesame oil. Set aside. (I prefer to make extra quantities of this and keep it in a squeeze bottle in the fridge.)

Fry each of the zucchini, carrot, enoki and shiitake separately in a little sesame oil over high heat until tender, seasoning with salt.

Cold-bowl bibimbap: If using ordinary bowls, fry the eggs sunny side up. Place 1½–2 cups of rice each into four bowls and arrange the separate toppings – zucchini, carrot and mushrooms, Spicy Beansprout Salad and cucumber – over the top. Top with a fried egg and a little sauce, stir and eat.

Hot-stone-bowl bibimbap: Heat four stone bowls over an open flame until very hot. Add 1 tsp of sesame oil around the edges of the bowls and place 1½–2 cups of rice in each. Quickly arrange the toppings on top and crack an egg into the centre. Stir until the egg has mixed with the rice and cooked through. Serve with the sauce.

TIP
Try leaving out the beef mince for a vegetarian version.

SEAFOOD PAJEON

These delicious Korean pancakes are a favourite of mine. Slightly crispy on the outside but doughy in the centre, plump with prawns and squid and having the nutty flavour of browned spring onions – they go perfectly with a beer or a soju.

MAKES: 2 PANCAKES
PREP: 10 MINUTES / **STAND:** 10 MINUTES / **COOK:** 10 MINUTES

1 cup plain flour
2 tbsp potato flour or cornflour
2 eggs
¼ tsp salt
1¼ cups cold water
4–6 spring onions (about 250g), trimmed
4 tbsp sesame oil, or vegetable oil
1½ cups raw peeled prawns and squid,
   roughly chopped
¼ tsp toasted sesame seeds

DIPPING SAUCE

1 tbsp light soy sauce
2 tsp rice vinegar
1 tsp sesame oil
¼ tsp (preferably Korean) chilli powder
½ clove garlic, peeled and minced
¼ tsp sugar
A pinch of toasted sesame seeds

For the dipping sauce, mix all the ingredients together. (A small screw-top jar is great for this.) The amount of sauce is enough for this recipe, but I recommend making double or triple the quantity and keeping it in the fridge.

For the batter, lightly whisk together the flours, eggs, salt and 1¼ cups of cold water until just combined. A few lumps is fine. Stand in the fridge for at least 10 minutes before using.

Slice the spring onions thickly lengthways (in halves or quarters) and trim the ends so they will fit into a large frypan, touching as much of the pan as possible. You can leave them whole if they are very thin.

Heat 1½ tablespoons of the sesame oil in a large frypan until very hot and place half of the spring onions in the pan in one layer and in one direction. Scatter over half of the chopped seafood, fitting it into any gaps between the onions. Pour over the batter to cover all the onions and seafood, partially cover the pan (to allow steam to escape but keep heat in), and cook over medium heat for 3–4 minutes, or until golden brown and crisp underneath. Flip the pancake over and add another ½ tablespoon of sesame oil around the edges. Cook for about 3 minutes, or until golden. Repeat for a second pancake.

Transfer the pancakes to a cutting board and cut into large squares. Scatter with sesame seeds and serve with the dipping sauce.

TIP

Instead of seafood, you can use thinly sliced pork, kimchi, or both, or even leave it out for a vegetarian version.

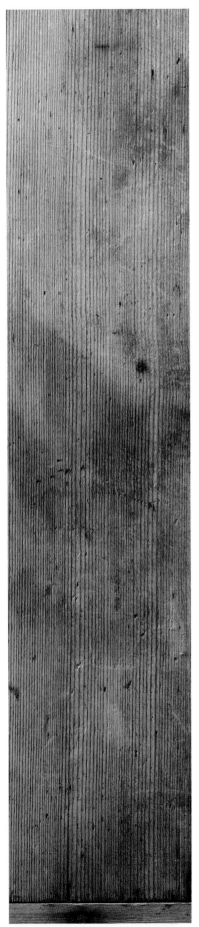

These delicious buns take a cue from a Vietnamese favourite, banh mi. When I first made these with my friend Callum for a big group, they were a hit. Containing a simple selection of toppings, the buns are fast to prepare and a star performer whenever you have a crowd to feed.

DUCK BUNS

MAKES: 8 BUNS
PREP: 10 MINUTES / **COOK:** 10 MINUTES / **STAND:** 5 MINUTES

2 large duck breasts, skin on
¼ cup hoisin sauce
8 small soft white rolls
Japanese mayonnaise, to serve
Sriracha chilli sauce, to serve
1 continental cucumber, peeled and thinly sliced
1 cup mint leaves, loosely packed
1 cup coriander leaves, loosely packed
1 cup Pickled Carrot & Daikon (page 30)

Brush the meat side of the duck breasts with a little hoisin sauce and put them, skin-side down, in a cold frypan. Place the pan over medium heat for about 7–8 minutes to allow the fat to render and the skin to crisp. Turn over and cook the meat side for 3 minutes, or until cooked to your liking. Rest for 5 minutes, then slice thinly.

While the duck is resting, split the buns in half almost all the way through and toast the insides under a grill until golden brown.

To assemble the buns, spread a little more hoisin sauce over one face of the bun and a little mayonnaise and chilli sauce on the other. Start with a few slices of cucumber and a few slices of duck. Add the mint, coriander and Pickled Carrot & Daikon. Repeat for the rest of the buns, and serve.

TIP
To save cooking time, you can substitute the duck breast with pieces of roast duck from a Cantonese barbecue shop.

This dish is hugely popular in Japanese lunch sets, and I used to order it almost once a week from a very stylish café just near my office in Tokyo. Whether for lunch or dinner, with just a bit of rice and a bowl of miso soup on the side, this makes for a fantastic and simple meal.

GINGER-FRIED PORK

SERVES: 4
PREP: 10 MINUTES / **MARINATE:** 30 MINUTES / **COOK:** 10 MINUTES

800g piece pork belly, skin and bones removed,
    thinly sliced to about ½cm
1 cup Light Teriyaki (page 32)
2 tbsp grated ginger, including juice
1 brown onion, peeled and thinly sliced
2 tsp peanut oil, or other vegetable oil
2 cups finely shredded cabbage, to serve
Chilli powder, to serve (optional)
Japanese mayonnaise, to serve

Mix the pork together with all the ingredients except the oil and leave to marinate for 30 minutes. Remove the pork slices, retaining the marinade.

Heat the oil over high heat in a large frypan and pan-fry the pork until lightly browned but not quite cooked through. Add the reserved marinade and bring to the boil, then simmer for about 3 minutes, tossing until the pork is well coated, the onions are slightly softened and the sauce has thickened.

Allow the pork to rest for just a minute off the heat, then serve with a mound of shredded cabbage sprinkled with chilli powder, and a little mayonnaise.

TIP
Try this marinade for barbecuing thicker pork chops, cutlets or pork neck steaks.

MALAYSIAN BARBECUE FISH

I love recipes in which ingredients can just be thrown into a food processor to produce something spectacular. The intense fragrance of this simple fish sambal is an excellent example of creating complex flavours from simple processes.

SERVES: 4
PREP: 10 MINUTES / **MARINATE:** 30–60 MINUTES / **COOK:** 6 MINUTES / **REST:** 3 MINUTES

4 cutlets of firm white-fleshed fish, such as
    blue-eye trevala, ling or Spanish mackerel
1 tbsp vegetable oil
Cooked rice and lime wedges, to serve

SAMBAL

3 large red or golden shallots, peeled
3 large red chillies, deseeded
3 cloves garlic, peeled
2 thick slices (about 15g) ginger, peeled
1 stalk lemongrass, white part only
1 tsp ground turmeric
½ cup coconut milk
1 tsp caster sugar
1 tsp belacan, or 1½ tsp fish sauce
¼ tsp salt

Process the sambal ingredients in a food processor until a thick paste is formed. Put the fish in a large Ziploc bag and pour in the paste, mixing well to ensure the fish is fully coated. Marinate out of the fridge for 30–60 minutes.

Remove the fish from the sambal and transfer the sambal to a small saucepan. Bring the sambal to the boil, stirring constantly, and cook for 2 minutes.

Heat a barbecue or grill pan until very hot and brush with vegetable oil. Cook the fish for about 3 minutes on each side, brushing repeatedly with the sambal, until the fish is nearly cooked through. Remove from the grill and rest in a draught-free place for about 3 minutes.

Serve the fish with rice, a little more of the sambal on top, and a wedge of lime.

TIP
This sambal is also great on whole fish, which can be wrapped in banana leaves or aluminium foil and cooked on the barbecue.

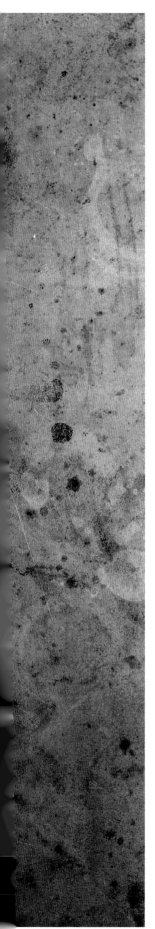
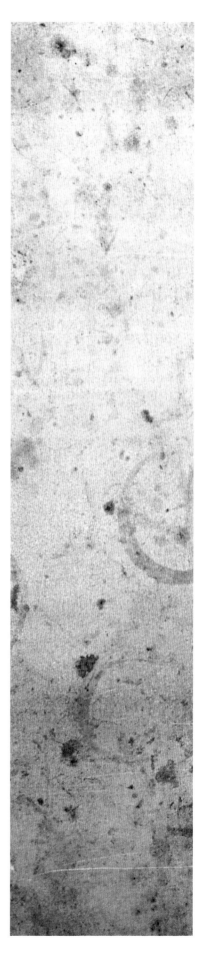

Kinilaw is a Filipino dish of raw seafood marinated in vinegar, similar to a ceviche. I prefer to make this with white fish, but you could use tuna, salmon, oysters or anything you like. Many recipes also call for the kinilaw to be marinated in the vinegar for many hours, but I find this a little too strong.

KINILAW

SERVES: 6–8 AS A SNACK
PREP: 10 MINUTES

500g sashimi-grade kingfish, tuna, swordfish, or
    any other good-quality fish
3 tbsp coconut vinegar, rice vinegar or white vinegar
Juice of 1 lime (about 25ml)
1 tsp grated ginger
2 bird's-eye chillies, thinly sliced
¼ red onion, peeled and finely diced
1 stalk spring onion, light green part only, thinly sliced
Sea salt, to taste
Thinly sliced cucumber, to serve

Cut the fish into 2cm cubes. Mix together with the remaining ingredients using your hands, and season with sea salt. Serve immediately with some thinly sliced cucumber.

TIP

If the fish smells 'fishy' rather than of seawater, rinse the cubed fish first in an additional 4 tbsp vinegar, pouring the vinegar off before you add the marinade.

As a variation to this recipe, try adding 2 tbsp coconut milk to the rest of the ingredients.

When sourcing ingredients, you can approach these recipes confident they won't be sending you into uncharted territory. I've deliberately chosen ingredients that are common, available and versatile.

PENANG ACHAR

I was born in Penang in Malaysia, and this Nyonya-style pickled vegetable dish is something my mother made often when we were growing up. As a child, the powerful flavours were too strong for my young tastes, but now I love it as a side dish, a salad or a snack.

MAKES: ABOUT 800 GRAMS
PREP: 20 MINUTES / **COOK:** 1 HOUR 10 MINUTES / **REFRIGERATE:** OVERNIGHT

500ml white vinegar
1 tsp salt, plus ½ tsp extra
1 tsp sugar, plus ½ tsp extra
1 cup water
1 continental cucumber, deseeded and cut into batons
2 carrots, cut into batons
150g cauliflower, broken into small florets
80g green beans, topped and tailed and cut into 2cm lengths
¼ head of cabbage, core removed and cut into 2cm slices
3 long red chillies, sliced on the diagonal
2 tbsp peanut oil, or other vegetable oil
1 tbsp toasted sesame seeds
4 tbsp roughly chopped roasted peanuts

REMPAH

3–4 shallots, or 1 brown onion, peeled and roughly chopped
1 clove garlic
1 tsp grated ginger
1 stalk lemongrass, white part only (optional)
1 tsp ground turmeric
½ tsp chilli powder
1 tsp belacan, or 1½ tsp fish sauce

Place the vinegar in a non-reactive saucepan with the salt, sugar and 1 cup of water, and bring to the boil. Blanch the vegetables separately in this liquid, for about 1 minute each, removing the batches with a slotted spoon and draining well. Place the vegetables on a large baking tray in the sun, or bake in a very low oven (around 50°C) for 1 hour. (If you prefer, you can skip this drying step.) Reserve the blanching liquid.

Pound the ingredients for the rempah in a mortar and pestle, or process in a food processor to a smooth paste. You can add a little water if the food processor is not catching the ingredients.

Heat the oil in a wok or small saucepan over high heat and fry the paste for 3–4 minutes, or until it is fragrant and cooked through, then add ½ a cup of the blanching liquid and bring to the boil. Remove from the heat.

Place the vegetables in a large bowl. Wearing gloves, mix the fried rempah through the vegetables, along with the sesame seeds, peanuts and an additional ½ tsp each of salt and sugar. Pack the vegetables into jars or plastic containers and refrigerate overnight before eating.

TIP

Try adding 100g of fresh pineapple pieces to the vegetables for a sweeter version.

This is my favourite way to cook ocean trout because it's simple, quick and perfect every time. As a dish, this ticks all the after-work boxes of being easy, fast, healthy and delicious, and I think it's one you'll keep coming back to again and again.

OCEAN TROUT WITH GARLIC & SOY

SERVES: 4 (OR MORE AS PART OF A SHARED MEAL)
PREP: 5 MINUTES / **COOK:** 12 MINUTES / **REST:** 2 MINUTES

1 whole side of ocean trout
½ tsp salt flakes
¼ tsp white pepper
Lemon cheeks, to serve

GARLIC & SOY SAUCE
1 tsp extra-virgin olive oil
3 cloves garlic, peeled and roughly chopped
½ tsp caster sugar
3 tbsp light soy sauce, or Umami Sauce (page 29)

Heat the oven to 200°C (fan-forced) and line a tray with baking paper. Lightly oil the baking paper, place the trout skin-side down on the tray and scatter with the salt and white pepper. You don't need to rub the salt and pepper into the fish. Bake for 10–12 minutes and rest for a further 2 minutes before serving.

To make the sauce, heat the olive oil in a small frypan over medium heat and fry the garlic until it starts to brown. Add the caster sugar and continue to fry until the garlic is golden brown. Remove from the heat, pour the soy sauce into the pan and stir until the sugar is dissolved.

Serve the ocean trout on the baking paper, and when eating, separate the flesh from the skin. It should come away very easily. Discard the skin. Serve with lemon cheeks and the garlic and soy sauce on the side.

TIP
Substitute the ocean trout for salmon fillets, if you prefer.

Fish cooked this way can be easily flaked and tossed through a salad or pasta.

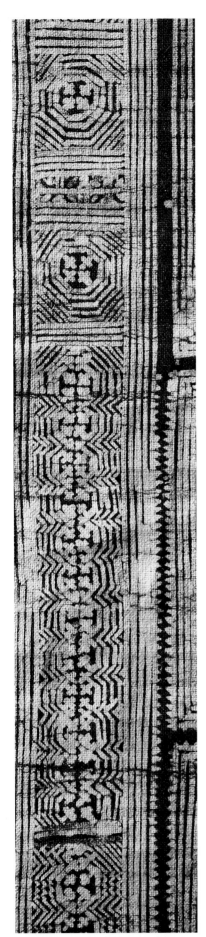

On a hot summer's night can you think of anything better than a big bowl of prawns and a beer? Serve this with a salad for a full meal, or just enjoy the prawns as they are. This is the kind of dish that makes a mid-week barbecue a family hit.

GRILLED PRAWNS WITH SALTY LIME

SERVES: 2 (OR 4 AS A SNACK)
PREP: 10 MINUTES / **COOK:** 4 MINUTES

---

12 large raw king prawns, peeled and deveined, tails on
1 tsp peanut oil, or other vegetable oil
Bird's-eye chillies, sliced (optional)

SALTY LIME
1 tsp salt flakes
4 Sichuan peppercorns (optional)
A few grinds of black pepper
A pinch of caster sugar
2 limes, cut into wedges

To make the salty lime, toast the salt and Sichuan peppercorns (if using) in a dry frypan until fragrant. Grind in a mortar and pestle along with the black pepper and sugar. Set aside.

Heat the barbecue or grill pan until very hot. Toss the prawns in the oil and grill for 2–3 minutes each side, or until the prawns are just opaque. Don't overcook the prawns – this is the most important part of the dish.

Place the prawns in a big bowl and put a pile of the salt and pepper mixture in a smaller dish. If using, scatter a few slices of fresh chilli over the salt. Squeeze the juice from the lime wedges over the salt mixture to partially dissolve it, and dip the prawns in the salty lime as you eat them.

TIP
If you don't mind peeling the prawns as you eat them (or eating the shells), grilling prawns in the shell will give you a little more flavour. Just split the shell to remove the intestinal tract and trim the prawn head just behind the eyes before grilling.

SWEET & SOUR PORK

Sweet and sour pork gets a bad rap for being a non-authentic, 'Westernised' imitation of Chinese food, but it is actually a very authentic dish in Cantonese cuisine. This version combines big chunks of pork and vegetables in a delicious sauce that can just as easily place you in Guangdong as it can your local Chinese takeaway.

SERVES: 4 (OR MORE AS PART OF A SHARED MEAL)
PREP: 15 MINUTES / **COOK:** 15 MINUTES

500g pork neck, cut into 2cm cubes
½ cup cornflour
Vegetable oil for deep-frying
1 small carrot, peeled and cut into irregular chunks
1 brown onion, peeled and cut into large cubes
150g fresh pineapple, cubed
1 Lebanese cucumber, cut into irregular chunks
2 tomatoes, cut into wedges
1 red capsicum, deseeded and cut into large squares
Cooked rice, to serve

SWEET & SOUR SAUCE

½ cup rice vinegar
¼ cup Shaoxing wine
¼ cup caster sugar
3 tbsp light soy sauce
1 tbsp tomato sauce
1 tsp sea salt
3 cloves garlic, peeled and crushed
1 tbsp grated ginger

Toss the pork in the cornflour to coat. Heat the oil to 180°C in a wide saucepan or wok. Deep-fry the pork for 2–3 minutes, or until well browned but not cooked through. Remove to drain on a wire rack.

Mix together all of the sauce ingredients in a wok and bring to a simmer over high heat. Add the carrot, onion and pineapple and simmer, covered, for 5 minutes, or until the carrot starts to soften. Add the pork, cucumber, tomato and capsicum and simmer for a further 5 minutes, until the vegetables are softened and the pork is cooked through. If necessary, thicken the sauce with a little cornflour mixed with cold water. Serve with rice.

TIP

I prefer my sweet and sour pork with just a thin coating of cornflour rather than a heavy batter, because that's how we ate it at home. If you prefer a battered version, a simple batter of self-raising flour, cornflour, egg and water works well.

PINEAPPLE FRIED RICE

As a kid, I loved the theatre of pineapple fried rice coming to the table served in a big, hollowed-out pineapple. This way of serving it is not so common at Australian Thai restaurants these days, but whenever I visit Thailand I'm sure to order it at least once, just for nostalgia's sake.

SERVES: 4
PREP: 15 MINUTES / **COOK:** 10 MINUTES

---

3 tbsp peanut oil, or other vegetable oil
200g chicken thighs, skinless, sliced
200g fresh pineapple, cut into small chunks
150g raw prawns, peeled and deveined
½ cup frozen peas
¼ cup roasted, unsalted cashews
2 tbsp raisins
2 tbsp fish sauce
1 tbsp soy sauce
1 tsp curry powder
8 cups cooked jasmine rice
Salt, to taste
2 spring onions, trimmed and sliced
A handful of coriander leaves, to serve
Fried shallots, to serve (optional)

Heat the oil in a wok over high heat and fry the chicken for a minute or so. Add the pineapple and fry until starting to caramelise. Add the prawns, peas, cashews and raisins and fry until the prawns change colour, then add the fish sauce, soy sauce and curry powder and stir to combine. Toss through the rice, pressing it firmly against the side of the wok to break up any clumps and to ensure it fries well. Taste a spoonful and add salt or a little more fish sauce if required.

Toss through the spring onions and serve scattered with coriander and fried shallots, if using.

TIP

If you want to serve this in a hollowed-out pineapple, I prefer to first roast the pineapple in a very hot oven for 20 minutes to caramelise some of the sugars and also to keep the fried rice warm at the table.

YUM CHA MANGO PANCAKES

The sight of these guys coming around on the trolley brings a smile to the face of any yum cha diner. You can roll them well in advance and keep them in the fridge until ready to serve. I prefer to dye the pancakes with saffron, but use food colouring if you prefer, or even just leave them uncoloured.

MAKES: 12–15 PANCAKES
PREP: 15 MINUTES / **STAND:** 30 MINUTES / **COOK:** 15 MINUTES / **CHILL:** 40 MINUTES

300ml thickened cream
4 tbsp icing sugar
3 ripe mangoes

PANCAKE BATTER
6 eggs
4 tbsp caster sugar
1 cup milk
1 cup (100g) plain flour
½ tsp salt
1 tsp vanilla extract
A few strands of saffron, soaked in 2 tsp water,
    or 2 drops yellow food colouring (optional)
4 tbsp vegetable oil

For the batter, whisk together the eggs and sugar then add the milk. In a separate bowl, sift together the flour and salt and whisk into the egg and milk mixture a little at a time. Add the vanilla extract, oil and saffron water or food colouring, and stir to combine. Push the mixture through a sieve to remove any lumps, cover and allow to stand for 30 minutes at room temperature. The mixture should be quite watery.

Heat a large non-stick frypan over low heat. If you have a good non-stick pan you don't need to add any oil, otherwise brush the pan with a very thin layer of oil. Pour in a little of the batter and tilt the pan to create a very thin pancake. Cover the pan and cook for 3 minutes, or until the top is firm. (You don't need to flip the pancakes and you don't want to brown the base too much.) Transfer to a plate and repeat for the rest of the batter. Cover the pancakes with cling film and chill in the fridge for 30 minutes.

Whip the cream and icing sugar until the cream holds a peak. Peel the mangoes (cut off the cheeks and remove the skin with a large spoon) and slice the flesh thickly.

Spoon or pipe a little whipped cream onto the fried side of each pancake and top with two slices of mango. Cover the mango with a little more cream and roll the pancake up like a spring roll. Chill in the fridge for at least 10 minutes before serving.

TIP
Try this with other fruits. You could even make a rainbow of pancakes by separating the batter and dyeing each batch with food colouring to match the filling.

SWEET ALMOND PUDDING WITH POACHED APRICOTS

This Chinese dessert was traditionally made by setting sweetened 'milk' from ground apricot kernels with agar agar, a seaweed-based setting agent. It's much easier and faster nowadays, using milk, almond essence and gelatin. Although none of the original ingredients are the same, the flavour is fantastic and there's still a nod to its beginnings with sweet poached apricots to complete the dish. This is a great dinner party dessert because it takes just minutes to prepare, can sit in the fridge until ready to serve, and looks spectacular coming to the table.

SERVES: 6

PREP: 5 MINUTES / **COOK:** 15 MINUTES / **REFRIGERATE:** 2 HOURS

18g powdered gelatin
1 litre full-cream milk
½ cup caster sugar
2 tsp almond essence

POACHED APRICOTS

1 cup sugar
2 cups water
6 fresh apricots, peeled and halved
1 tbsp goji berries (optional)

Sprinkle the gelatin over 250ml of the milk and leave to bloom for 5 minutes. Heat the remaining milk, caster sugar and almond essence over medium heat until the sugar is dissolved, then whisk through the gelatin–milk mixture over heat until completely dissolved. Strain into six bowls or glasses and chill in the fridge for 1–2 hours, until well set.

For the poached apricots, bring the sugar and water to the boil to make a simple syrup. Add the apricot halves and goji berries, if using, and simmer for 10 minutes, or until the apricots are tender. Allow to cool in the syrup. Serve the apricots on top of the almond pudding.

TIP

I prefer powdered gelatin over leaf gelatin for most home cooking because it is easier to measure, and if you stick to the same brand you don't have to worry about calculating bloom strength as for leaf gelatin. Some people say leaf gelatin produces a clearer jelly, but in this case it doesn't matter at all.

SATURDAY

PAN SUSHI

Hawaiian cuisine has influences from all over the world, and they've been adapted to the relaxed island style. One of my favourite Hawaiian innovations is pan sushi. Not everyone can make sushi like the pros, and this excellent, simple kind of sushi is perfect for feeding a crowd.

MAKES: ABOUT 24 PIECES
PREP: 10 MINUTES / **COOK:** 45 MINUTES / **STAND:** 30 MINUTES

300g canned tuna in oil, drained
3 tbsp Light Teriyaki (page 32)
2 tsp Chilli Furikake (page 33)
3–4 sheets nori
2 avocados, peeled and sliced
3 tbsp red Japanese pickled ginger (benishouga), drained

SUSHI RICE
125ml rice vinegar
50g caster sugar
5g salt
4 cups short-grain rice

Fry the drained tuna in a frypan for a minute or so, stirring constantly. Add the Light Teriyaki and continue to fry until all the liquid is gone. Allow to cool to room temperature.

For the sushi rice, place the vinegar, caster sugar and salt in a small saucepan and stir over low heat until the sugar and salt dissolve. Allow to cool to room temperature. Cook the rice in accordance with the instructions for Two-To-One Rice on page 40, and transfer the hot rice to a very large bowl. Fan the rice to drive off any excess moisture and gradually add the vinegar mixture, stirring the rice with a spatula using a cutting motion. Continue to fan and stir the rice until it reaches body temperature. Divide into three equal portions.

Line a deep 25cm square baking tray with baking paper (allowing the paper to overhang the edges of the pan) and scatter the paper with Chilli Furikake. With wet hands, evenly spread one portion of rice over the furikake and then cover the rice with a single layer of nori (shiny side down), trimming the nori as necessary. Each layer of nori in the sushi will require more than 1 sheet. Place a layer of avocado slices over the nori and cover with another portion of rice. Scatter over the pickled ginger and spread the tuna mix over the ginger. Top with the final portion of rice and another layer of nori (shiny side up). Cover with another layer of baking paper, press down firmly all over and allow to stand for at least 30 minutes, preferably with a weight on top.

Remove the top baking paper layer, place a large cutting board over the pan and, in one motion, invert the pan so that the sushi is on the cutting board. Carefully remove the remaining baking paper. With a wet knife, cut into individual portions, being sure to cut all the way through the bottom sheet of nori.

TIP
You can use any fillings you like. Instead of frying the tuna with the teriyaki sauce, try mixing Japanese mayonnaise and Sriracha chilli sauce through drained tuna for a spicy tuna mix.

DRY-BAKED LAMB CHOP CURRY WITH SWEET POTATO

At one time when I was growing up, my mother had six kids in school and one in day-care, she was working full time, and she still managed to come home and prepare dinner for the entire crowd. Her dry lamb chop curry is one of my best childhood memories. My eternal thanks, Mum, and thanks to mothers everywhere.

SERVES: 4
PREP: 15 MINUTES / **MARINATE:** 30 MINUTES / **COOK:** 40 MINUTES

1.5kg lamb forequarter chops
1 large orange-fleshed sweet potato
2 red onions, peeled and cut into eighths
1 tsp vegetable oil
Salt, to taste
Yoghurt, to serve
A handful of coriander leaves, to serve
Cooked rice, to serve

CURRY RUB
2 tbsp ghee or vegetable oil
Juice of ½ lemon
1 tbsp honey
2 tsp sea salt
2 cloves garlic, peeled and grated
1½ tsp grated ginger
1 tbsp light soy sauce
1 tbsp sesame oil
1 tsp freshly ground black pepper
1 tsp ground turmeric
1 tsp ground coriander
1 tsp ground cumin
A handful of curry leaves, bruised (optional)

Combine the curry rub ingredients and mix together with the lamb chops, rubbing in well. Marinate for at least 30 minutes at room temperature, or overnight in the fridge.

Heat the oven to 180°C (fan-forced). Peel the sweet potato with a vegetable peeler and discard the peel. Continue peeling into long ribbons. Toss the sweet potato ribbons and onion in the oil and season with salt.

Line the base of a large baking tray (or two separate trays if you don't have a large tray) with baking paper and arrange the lamb chops in a single layer. Place the onions and sweet potato in between the chops. Bake for 30–40 minutes (turning the lamb halfway through cooking), until the lamb is cooked through and the vegetables are slightly charred.

Transfer everything to a serving platter, drizzle with a little yoghurt and scatter with coriander. Serve with rice.

TIP
If you prefer your lamb chops pink in the middle, bake the onions and sweet potato separately and cook the lamb chops on a grill. Top the chops with the onion and sweet potato to serve.

SUGARCANE PRAWN ROLLS

It's wonderful having a huge platter of fresh, delicious ingredients put in front of you and spending a leisurely dinner putting together your own meal and eating your fill. These prawn skewers can be made well in advance, ready for some simple grilling or frying. As an added bonus, having people make their own rolls is a great timesaver.

SERVES: 4

PREP: 20 MINUTES / **COOK:** 20 MINUTES

100g dried rice vermicelli, to serve
Whole butter lettuce leaves or shredded iceberg lettuce, to serve
Pickled Carrot & Daikon (page 30), to serve (optional)
A handful of mint leaves, to serve
A handful of coriander leaves, to serve
About 15 dried rice paper rounds, to serve

PRAWN PASTE

600g raw prawn meat, roughly chopped
1 tbsp fish sauce
1 tsp caster sugar
1 shallot, peeled
1 clove garlic, peeled
6 sticks sugarcane, about 15–20cm long and 1cm square

COLD ROLL SAUCE

2 tbsp hoisin sauce
2 tbsp water
1 tbsp Sriracha chilli sauce
1 clove garlic, peeled and finely chopped
1 tsp fish sauce
1 tbsp lime juice
2 tbsp crushed roasted peanuts

For the prawn paste, combine all the ingredients except the sugarcane in a food processor and process to a smooth paste. With wet hands, mould the paste around lengths of sugarcane. Steam the skewers for 8 minutes, until cooked through, and set aside. (Sugarcane is available fresh from some fruit and vegetable suppliers, or in cans from Asian grocers. You can also mould the prawn paste around sticks of lemongrass, metal skewers or even just form them into balls.)

To prepare the rice vermicelli, place in a heatproof bowl and pour over boiling water until completely submerged. Stir occasionally for about 2–3 minutes, until the vermicelli is cooked through (taste to make sure), then run under cold water and drain well. Set aside.

For the cold roll sauce, mix together all the ingredients. As an alternative to this sauce, you can use nuoc cham sauce (page 134).

When ready to serve, grill or fry the skewers until lightly charred and place them with the other ingredients, except the rice paper rounds, on a large platter, along with the cold roll sauce for dipping. Serve with a stack of rice paper and a large bowl (or multiple bowls) of warm water. To make the rolls, dip the rice paper into the water until just softening and then roll up with the ingredients of your choice.

TIP

If you don't want to make these into rolls, serve the skewers on top of some warm rice vermicelli noodles with sliced cucumber, Pickled Carrot & Daikon (page 30), mint, coriander, fried shallots and dress with nuoc cham sauce (page 134).

PORK & PRAWN WONTONS

The English word 'wonton' comes from the Cantonese pronunciation of the Chinese characters meaning 'swallowing clouds'. These little dumplings can contain any number of fillings, but in my opinion these pork and prawn ones are the best.

MAKES: ABOUT 50 WONTONS
PREP: 45 MINUTES / **REST:** 45 MINUTES / **COOK:** 5 MINUTES

50 square wonton wrappers

FOR FRIED WONTONS
Vegetable oil for deep-frying (about 2 litres)
Your favourite chilli sauce, to serve

FOR BOILED WONTONS
Hot Chilli Oil (page 24)
Chinkiang black vinegar and chopped chives,
   to serve

FILLING
500g fatty pork mince (or 500g roughly chopped
   pork belly)
200g raw prawn meat, roughly chopped
3 large spring onions, white and light green parts,
   trimmed and finely chopped
1 tbsp minced ginger
2 cloves garlic, peeled and finely chopped
¼ tsp salt
1 tsp light soy sauce
1 tsp Shaoxing wine
½ tsp caster sugar

Using a wooden spoon or spatula, mix together the filling ingredients vigorously for about 5 minutes, stirring in one direction only. (Rather than a bowl, I prefer to use a large, heavy-based saucepan for this, as the handle and vertical sides make it easier to stir the heavy mixture.) Set aside to rest in the fridge for 30 minutes.

To make the wontons, refer to the illustrations on pages 216–217, and to the following instructions.

Take a wonton wrapper and moisten the edges with a finger dipped in cold water. Place a teaspoon of filling in the centre and fold two corners together to form a triangle, taking care to remove as much air as possible. Pinch the edges together firmly to create a sealed packet. Moisten one tip of the long side of the triangle and bring the other tip of the long end onto the moistened part. Pinch together firmly. Continue until all the filling is used up, then place the completed wontons on a tray lined with baking paper. Refrigerate for 15 minutes. If you are not cooking them immediately, put the tray of wontons in the freezer. When they are well frozen, transfer to a large freezer bag (taking care not to break the tips of the pastry). The frozen wontons can be boiled straight from the freezer for about 5 minutes until they are cooked through.

To cook the unfrozen wontons, you can deep-fry them in 170°C oil for 2–3 minutes until golden brown, or boil them in plenty of salted water for 4 minutes until soft and cooked through.

Serve the deep-fried wontons with chilli sauce, or dress boiled wontons with a little Hot Chilli Oil (page 24) and Chinkiang black vinegar, and scatter with chives. Alternatively, you can turn the boiled wontons into Short Soup (page 65) or Dry Wonton Noodles (page 122).

TIP
This same wonton filling can be used to make delicious Siu Mai dumplings (page 231).

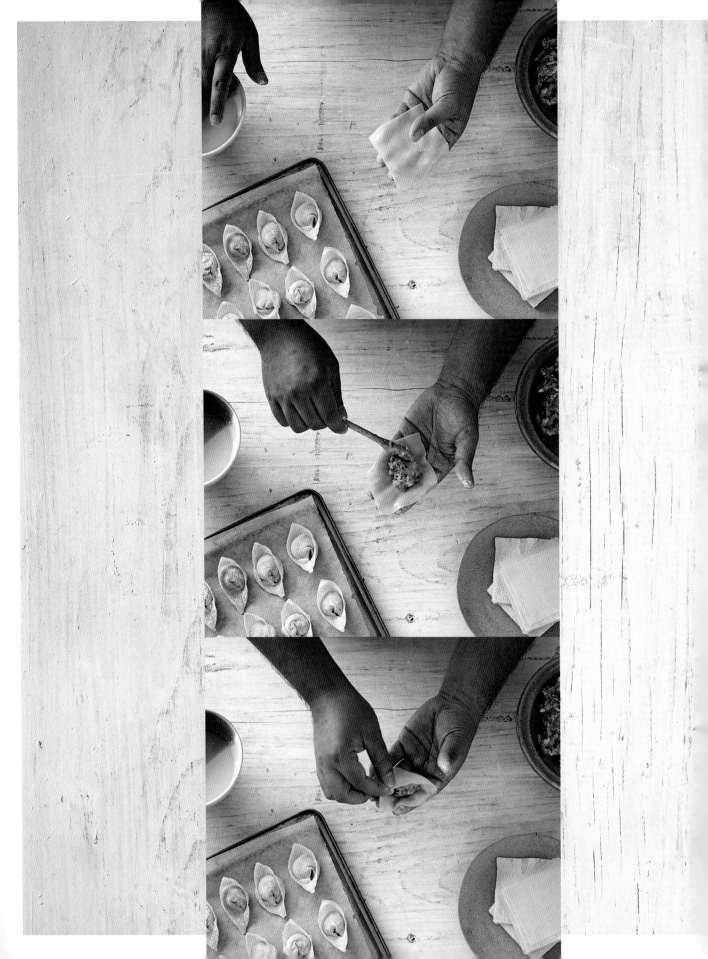

DUCK SHOYU RAMEN

If you've been to Japan, you know how soulful a hot bowl of ramen can be. The problem is that it usually takes hours, or even days to cook yourself. With a bit of forward planning, this duck version is ready in just minutes, and is the perfect solution to getting a home ramen fix.

SERVES: 4

PREP: 15 MINUTES / **COOK:** 20 MINUTES / **STEEP:** 1 HOUR

---

2 duck breasts, skin on
3 tbsp Light Teriyaki (page 32)
750g ramen noodles, fresh (soft, thin wheat or egg noodles)
2 tsp Garlic & Shallot Oil (page 21)
Thinly sliced spring onions, to serve
Toasted sesame seeds, to serve
1 sheet nori, cut into quarters

SOY BROTH

2 litres White Chicken Stock (page 20)
300ml Light Teriyaki (page 32)
4 cloves garlic, peeled and grated

STEEPED EGGS

4 eggs, at room temperature
500ml water
200ml Umami Sauce (page 29) or light soy sauce
1 tbsp dark soy sauce

To make the steeped eggs, place the eggs into vigorously boiling water for 6–8 minutes, depending on how firm you want the yolks, then place them in iced water to stop the cooking process. Peel the eggs and cover with the 500ml of water, Umami Sauce and dark soy sauce in a deep bowl. Leave submerged to steep for at least 1 hour.

Place the duck breasts skin-side down in a cold frypan. Place the pan over medium heat for about 7–8 minutes to allow the fat to render and the skin to crisp. Turn over and cook the meat side for 3 minutes, or until cooked to your liking. Add the Light Teriyaki and roll the duck breasts through the sauce until they are glazed and sticky. Rest for 5 minutes, then slice thinly.

For the soy broth, mix all the broth ingredients together and bring to a low simmer.

For the noodles, boil in plenty of boiling salted water for about 1 minute until tender, or according to packet instructions.

To assemble the ramen, place ½ tsp Garlic & Shallot Oil in the bottom of each of four large bowls. Ladle over 2 cups of the soy broth per bowl and distribute the noodles. Slice the eggs in half and place two halves on top of each bowl of noodles. Arrange equal portions of duck next to the egg, scatter over some spring onion and sesame seeds, and finish with a square of nori at the edge of each bowl.

TIP

Don't boil the noodles directly in the stock, as this will make your stock cloudy and thick from the flour. If you like, you can add additional flavours to the stock with shiitake mushrooms, or dried shrimp or scallops – experiment to find what you like.

As you look through the dishes in this book, think about how they might make their way into your own family menu. Just adding one or two to your repertoire can make a world of difference to your enjoyment of everyday meals.

VIETNAMESE BEEF STEW (BO KHO)

My grandmother doesn't eat beef, but when I was growing up she would often make us kids the most delicious beef stew, testing the meat with a skewer rather than tasting a piece. Looking back, the fact that she was cooking something for us that she couldn't eat herself has taught me a lot about how cooking really is an expression of love.

SERVES: 6

PREP: 15 MINUTES / **COOK:** 2 HOURS / **STAND:** 15 MINUTES

1.5kg chuck steak, cut into 4cm cubes
2 tbsp plain flour
1 tbsp paprika
Salt, to taste
¼ cup peanut oil, or other vegetable oil
½ cup tomato paste
3 thick slices ginger
1 brown onion, peeled and finely chopped
3 cloves garlic, peeled and finely chopped
1 tsp Chinese five-spice powder
2 tsp curry powder
3 whole star anise
1 cinnamon quill
1 tsp cloves
2 stalks lemongrass, trimmed and bruised
2 bay leaves
2 litres low-salt beef stock
2 tbsp fish sauce
½ tsp salt
3 potatoes, peeled and cut into large chunks
3 carrots, peeled and cut into large chunks
Lime wedges, to serve
Red onion rings, to serve
A handful of coriander leaves, to serve
A handful of basil leaves, to serve
French-style baguettes, to serve

Toss the beef in the flour and paprika and season with a little salt. Heat the oil in a heavy casserole dish and fry the beef over medium heat (in batches if necessary) until it is well browned. Add the tomato paste, ginger, onion and garlic and stir for 2–3 minutes, or until the onion starts to turn translucent. Add the five-spice powder, curry powder, star anise, cinnamon, cloves, lemongrass and bay leaves and stir to combine. Pour in enough beef stock to cover the meat completely, add the fish sauce and salt and bring to a simmer. Simmer, covered, for about 1½ hours (skimming the top at regular intervals to remove any scum), or until the beef is just tender.

Add the potatoes and carrots and simmer for a further 10–15 minutes, until the vegetables soften. Allow to stand for about 15 minutes before serving.

Adjust the seasoning with salt or fish sauce, and serve with lime wedges, thinly sliced red onion, coriander and basil leaves and pieces of baguette to dip into the rich sauce.

TIP

Cooking onion and star anise together produces wonderful savoury flavours. Look out for this combination in recipes, because it's a great one.

With stir-fries, fried rice or noodle dishes, it's best to show a bit of restraint. Rather than ten different flavours clamouring for attention, these kinds of meals are often best with just a few simple ingredients, so their true flavours can shine. This fried rice will live or die by the quality of the crab meat you choose. If you can boil and pick the crab yourself, all the better.

CRAB & LETTUCE FRIED RICE

SERVES: 4

PREP: 15 MINUTES / **COOK:** 5 MINUTES

2 tbsp Garlic & Shallot Oil (page 21), or vegetable oil
1½ tbsp Liaw Family XO Sauce (page 22)
4 cups cooked rice
1 tbsp light soy sauce
1 tsp sea salt
A pinch of white pepper
2 eggs
2–3 spring onions, thinly sliced
150g picked crab meat
½ head of iceberg lettuce, thinly shredded

Heat the oil in a wok over high heat and add the Liaw Family XO Sauce. Add the rice, soy sauce, salt and pepper and toss to coat in the oil, pressing the rice against the edges of the wok to break up any clumps. Move the rice to one side and crack the eggs into the open side of the wok. Break the yolks and mix the egg until nearly set, then add the spring onion. Stir the eggs and onion through the rice.

Remove the wok from the heat and scatter over the crab meat and the lettuce, tossing until the lettuce is wilted and well distributed. Season to taste, and serve.

TIP
Try this with chunks of cooked lobster for a decadent course in a special-occasion banquet.

BLACK PEPPER BEEF

Black pepper beef is a simple Cantonese favourite. Cooking the ingredients separately and combining them at the end is a valuable technique in Cantonese wok cookery; it preserves the heat of the wok and avoids overcrowding.

SERVES: 4 (OR MORE AS PART OF A SHARED MEAL)
PREP: 15 MINUTES / **COOK:** 5–10 MINUTES

500g beef rump, topside or Scotch fillet,
    thinly sliced
3–4 tbsp peanut oil, or other vegetable oil
2 cloves garlic, peeled and roughly chopped
1 tsp grated ginger
1 medium-sized brown onion, peeled and sliced
1 green capsicum, deseeded and thinly sliced
Cooked rice, to serve

MARINADE
1 tsp sesame oil
2 tsp cornflour
2 tsp light soy sauce
1 tbsp Shaoxing wine

BLACK PEPPER PASTE
1 tsp freshly ground black pepper
1 tbsp oyster sauce
1 tsp light soy sauce
¼ tsp caster sugar

Mix together the sliced beef and the marinade ingredients and set aside. Mix together the black pepper paste ingredients and set aside.

Heat a wok over high heat and pour 2 tbsp of the oil around the edges. Fry the beef (in batches if necessary) until browned but not quite cooked through. Remove from the wok and set aside.

Pour the remaining oil into the wok, add the garlic and ginger and fry over high heat for about 30 seconds, or until the garlic is starting to colour. Add the onion and capsicum and stir-fry for 2 minutes, until softened. Remove the vegetables from the wok and set aside.

Return the wok to high heat and add the beef (and any collected juices). Spoon in the black pepper paste and toss the beef for 2–3 minutes, until well coated and the paste is starting to caramelise. Return the vegetables to the wok, toss until well combined and serve with rice.

TIP
This recipe has a surprising amount of heat from the black pepper. For a milder version, reduce the amount of pepper in the paste and grind a little over at the end for flavour and aroma. This recipe also works well with pork or chicken.

DRAGON WINGS

The delicious sauce in this recipe is made by whisking all the ingredients together over heat. Cheap and easy to put together, it is one of my favourite recipes for when friends come around to watch the football.

SERVES: 6
PREP: 10 MINUTES / **COOK:** 40 MINUTES

1.5kg chicken wings (about 12–15 wings)
1 tsp caster sugar
1 tsp salt
1 tbsp vegetable oil

DRAGON WING SAUCE
75g unsalted butter
4 tbsp Sriracha chilli sauce
3 tbsp tomato sauce
2 tbsp rice wine vinegar
½ tsp Worcestershire sauce
¼ tsp mustard powder
¼ tsp onion powder
1 tsp caster sugar

AVOCADO DIP
1 ripe avocado
3 tbsp mayonnaise
1 tbsp sour cream
1 tbsp lemon juice
Salt, to taste

Heat the oven to 220°C (fan-forced). Cut the wings through the joints into three parts – drumettes, wingettes and wing-tips. Keep the wing-tips for stock and place the drumettes and wingettes in a bowl. Toss in the sugar, salt and oil.

Lay some baking paper on a large oven tray and arrange the wings in a single layer over the baking paper. Roast the wings for 25–30 minutes, turning once, until browned and crispy. (If you prefer, you can dust the wings in a little cornflour and deep-fry them.)

To make the Dragon Wing sauce, whisk together all the sauce ingredients in a saucepan over high heat until well combined and just simmering. Remove from the heat and toss the wings in the sauce until coated.

To make the avocado dip, combine all the dip ingredients in a food processor and process until smooth. Dilute with a little water or milk until it is a pourable consistency, taste and adjust the seasoning with salt. You can serve this cooling dip on the side, or if you prefer, transfer it into a squeeze bottle and drizzle over the wings before serving.

TIP
Make a double quantity of the Dragon Wing sauce and keep it in the fridge or freezer, ready to use whenever you like. It will keep for ages.

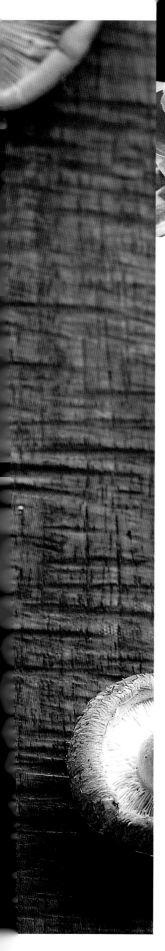

These little dumplings are my favourite at yum cha. Back at home, with a freezer full of these, you are never more than a few minutes away from a snack or a meal.

SIU MAI

MAKES: 24 DUMPLINGS
PREP: 1 HOUR / **REFRIGERATE:** 30 MINUTES / **COOK:** 8 MINUTES

4 dried shiitake mushrooms
Pork & Prawn Wontons filling (page 214) (chopped pork belly filling is preferable, but pork mince is also fine)
24 square wonton wrappers
½ carrot, peeled and finely diced
Liaw Family XO Sauce (page 22), Hot Chilli Oil (page 24), chilli sauce or soy sauce, to serve

Soak the dried mushrooms in hot water for 30 minutes, drain and finely dice. Stir into the wonton filling.

Using a circular pastry cutter, cut a circle from the square wonton wrapper. Take the round wonton wrapper and, with a butter knife or small spatula, place a small amount of filling in the centre. Gather the pastry around the filling and continue adding more, pushing the filling down tightly to ensure there are no air bubbles. Once the wrapper is gathered into a filled cylinder shape, push a single dice of carrot into the centre. Repeat until all the filling is used. Place the dumplings on a tray lined with baking paper and place in the fridge for at least 30 minutes before cooking. (The dumplings can also be frozen on the tray and then transferred to a large freezer bag.)

Sit a steamer over boiling water and steam the Siu Mai for 8 minutes (12 if from frozen). Serve with Liaw Family XO Sauce, Hot Chilli Oil, other chilli sauce or soy sauce for dipping.

COCONUT & TAMARIND PORK BELLY

This lovely, rich, caramelised pork belly dish is served without skin, so you don't need to worry about the crackling. Tamarind is a great souring agent for marinades and sauces. If using tamarind pulp with seeds instead of tamarind purée, double the quantity of tamarind and mix with hot water, squeezing to dissolve the pulp and separate the seeds.

SERVES: 4

PREP: 25 MINUTES / **MARINATE:** 1 HOUR / **COOK:** 1 HOUR

1.2kg piece pork belly, deboned and skin removed, cut into 3cm strips
A handful of coriander leaves, to serve

COCONUT & TAMARIND MARINADE

1 large brown onion, peeled and sliced
5 cloves garlic, peeled and roughly chopped
3 large red chillies, deseeded and sliced
1 tbsp tamarind purée
200ml water
200ml fish sauce
200ml dark soy sauce
100g caster sugar
1 tbsp sesame oil
200ml coconut milk

For the marinade, combine all the ingredients except the coconut milk in a saucepan and bring to a simmer. Simmer, uncovered, for 15 minutes, or until reduced by one-third, then stir through the coconut milk. Cool and then mix with the pork belly. Leave to marinate for at least 1 hour (or preferably overnight).

Heat the oven to 180°C (fan-forced). Remove the pork from the marinade and roast the pork in a non-stick roasting pan for 45 minutes to 1 hour, turning often until well caramelised. Bring the reserved marinade to the boil and simmer for 5 minutes. Baste the pork with the marinade throughout cooking. Rest for 10 minutes, slice and drizzle with a little of the marinade.

TIP

Try tossing a few pieces of this pork through the Fresh Herb & Prawn Salad (page 138).

This Korean summer dish is halfway between a fruit salad and a punch. Whether you want to eat it or drink it, there's no doubt that it's perfect for a hot summer's afternoon.

HWACHAE

SERVES: 4–6
PREP: 20 MINUTES / **REFRIGERATE:** 10 MINUTES

½ seedless watermelon, well chilled
3 cups other mixed fruits, such as strawberries,
    rockmelon, lychee, starfruit, kiwifruit, apple and
    goji berries, well chilled
Juice of 1 lime
4 cups chilled ginger ale or fizzy lemonade
½ cup cranberry juice

Ball the watermelon with a melon baller (or cut into small chunks). Similarly, ball the mixed fruit or cut with a knife or decorative cutters. Place all the fruit in a large bowl and pour over the lime juice, mixing to ensure the fruit is well covered. (If using goji berries, soak them in the cranberry juice for about 15 minutes first.)

Pour the ginger ale or lemonade and the cranberry juice (with or without goji berries) over the fruit. Leave in the fridge for 10 minutes, then serve.

TIP
I don't want to say I encourage it, but just imagine for a moment how it might taste to add a bottle of Korean soju to this …

CHOCOLATE & BERRY HONEY TOAST

Honey toast is a popular dessert that is said to have originated in the karaoke parlours of Japan's Shibuya district, spreading to Taiwanese dessert bars and then across Asia. It is incredibly decadent and delicious, and considering that each honey toast is half a loaf of bread, perhaps this is one you might want to share. (But don't feel that you have to!)

SERVES: 2–4 (MAKES 2 HONEY TOASTS FOR SHARING)
PREP: 10 MINUTES / **COOK:** 10 MINUTES

1 loaf soft brioche or white bread, unsliced
150g unsalted butter

TOPPINGS
Good-quality chocolate syrup
Golden syrup or honey
Good-quality vanilla ice cream
Whipped cream
Fresh berries, such as strawberries, blueberries and blackberries
Good-quality dark chocolate, shaved

Heat the oven to 180°C (fan-forced). Cut the loaf in half and, with a small serrated knife, cut around the centre through the cut side about 1cm from the crust. Cut through the back of the crust to remove the centre from the bread 'box'. Cut the crustless centre into 3cm cubes. Repeat for the other half of the loaf.

Melt the butter in a microwave or small saucepan, then dip the bread cubes into the melted butter and set aside on a baking tray lined with baking paper. It doesn't matter if the bread cubes aren't completely coated in butter. Brush the inside of each box with the remaining melted butter. Bake the cubes and the boxes for about 10 minutes, or until golden brown.

While still warm, drizzle a little chocolate syrup and golden syrup or honey into each bread box, put the toasted cubes back into the boxes and, working quickly, top each filled box with ice cream, whipped cream and berries. Drizzle the whole lot with more chocolate syrup and golden syrup, shave over a little chocolate and serve immediately. Eat and smile.

TIP
You can use any combination of flavours and toppings you like. Think of this as a Japanese sundae.

Most of the ingredients in this book can be found in any ordinary Australian supermarket. Take a closer look at the Asian food section where you shop; you may be surprised by what you find.

GLOSSARY

Belacan A strong-smelling Malaysian dried fermented shrimp paste, often sold in firm cakes.

Benishouga A type of Japanese vinegar pickle made from fine strips of ginger, dyed red with red perilla leaves. Benishouga is different from the (often pink) pickled ginger served with sushi, although that is a good substitute.

Bonito flakes Called katsuobushi in Japanese, these are fine flakes made from dried, fermented and smoked bonito or skipjack tuna. They are a valuable source of umami in Japanese cooking.

Broken rice Long-grain rice pieces from grains that have been broken in the rice milling process. In cooking, broken rice has a drier and softer texture than whole grains.

Char siu (sometimes spelled 'char siew') A sweet, glazed Chinese barbecued pork dish. Char siu is available cooked and sliced from Cantonese-style barbecue restaurants.

Cheong Chan caramel sauce A thick, sweet and savoury version of treacle made from molasses, used in South-East Asian cooking. Substitute dark soy sauce.

Chinkiang black vinegar A variety of dark Chinese vinegar made from black glutinous rice.

Coconut vinegar A light vinegar made from fermented coconut water sometimes used in South-East Asian cooking. Substitute rice vinegar or white vinegar.

Gochujang A versatile Korean paste made from fermented chilli, glutinous rice and soybeans.

Fish sauce A pungent and umami-rich sauce made from fermented fish and commonly used in South-East Asian cooking. There are many different varieties.

Japanese mayonnaise Japanese varieties of mayonnaise, such as the Kewpie brand, have a more savoury flavour and thicker texture than Western mayonnaises.

Kimchi Often spicy, kimchi is a general term for Korean fermented pickled vegetables. Popular varieties of kimchi use Chinese cabbage (wombok) as their main ingredient.

Kombu Kombu is the Japanese term for varieties of edible dried kelp that are an important source of umami in Japanese cooking.

Lap cheong A variety of semi-dried Chinese pork sausages. Lap cheong are often high in fat and strongly flavoured, so are best used sparingly.

Mantou White, slightly sweet Chinese steamed buns, often stuffed with fillings and eaten both in sweet and savoury dishes. Filled and unfilled mantou are available in the freezer section of Asian grocers.

Nori The Japanese term for type of edible seaweed, often sold in dry squares and used to wrap sushi. Nori is popular in both Japanese and Korean cuisine.

Panko breadcrumbs Japanese flake-style breadcrumbs used as a coating for some deep-fried foods.

Shaoxing wine A Chinese style of fermented rice wine often used in cooking, although more refined varieties are sometimes drunk as a beverage.

Shiso The Japanese term for a peppery, minty Asian herb of the perilla family. Shiso has both green and red varieties. Although the green variety is more common in Japanese cooking, the red variety is used to dye pickles and as a garnish for sushi and sashimi.

Sichuan peppercorns An aromatic Chinese spice, not related to black pepper or chilli, with a flavour and aroma reminiscent of citrus, and which produces a mild tingling sensation on the tongue when eaten.

Sriracha chilli sauce A style of chilli sauce originating in eastern Thailand, although popular modern varieties from the United States differ greatly to the Thai versions. In this book 'Sriracha chilli sauce' refers to the modern American versions.

INDEX

A

adobo, chicken 39
affogato, Vietnamese 82
apricots, poached 204
Asami's cheesecake 53
asazuke 77
avocado
    dip 229
    prawn & avocado doria 101
    salmon & avocado donburi 142

B

Balinese roast pork belly with fresh sambal 36
bananas, Malaysian deep-fried (goreng pisang) 145
bang-bang chicken salad 58
bang-bang dressing 58
BBQ Genghis Khan 173
beansprout salad, spicy 112
béchamel, enriched 101
beef
    bibimbap 178
    black pepper 226
    bowls (gyudon) 125
    bulgogi 166
    crying tiger 133
    fillet steak with red miso butter 154
    Japanese beef curry 169
    korokke with miso-mustard mayonnaise 170
    minced beef mix (for bibimbap) 178
    XO beef & broccoli 61
bibimbap 178
bibimbap sauce 178
black pepper beef 226
black pepper paste 226
bo kho (Vietnamese beef stew) 222
brown rice congee with crab 129
bulgogi, beef 166
buns, duck 182
butter, red miso 154

C

caramelised lemongrass pork chops 134
carrot & daikon, pickled (do chua) 30
casserole, Korean pork & kimchi (kimchi chigae) 108
celery, crystal prawns with 137
cheat's claypot 107
cheesecake, Asami's 53
chicken
    adobo 39
    bang-bang chicken salad 58
    cheat's claypot 107
    dragon wings 229
    fat noodles 141
    fish sauce roast 126
    garlic & crispy lime leaves, with 115
    Japanese triple-fried (kara age) 121
    kra-pow 158
    master stock fried chicken & five-spice salt 161
    master stock poached chicken breast 81
    Nagoya-style chicken wings 165
    pineapple fried rice 200
    teriyaki 92
    white chicken stock 20
chilli
    furikake 33
    hot chilli oil (ra-yu) 24
    ponzu 96
    vinegar, in 49
chocolate & berry honey toast 238
coconut
    coconut & tamarind marinade 234
    coconut & tamarind pork belly 234
    lychee & coconut granita 116
    simplest coconut ice cream 146
condensed milk ice cream 82
crab & lettuce fried rice 225
crab, brown rice congee with 129
crispy squid with chilli furikake 95
crying tiger 133
crying tiger sauce 133

crystal prawns with celery 137
curry, dry-baked lamb chop with sweet potato 210
curry, Japanese beef 169
curry rub 210
curry salt 70

D

daikon & carrot, pickled (do chua) 30
desserts
  Asami's cheesecake 53
  chocolate & berry honey toast 238
  hwachae 237
  leche flan 50
  lychee & coconut granita 116
  Malaysian deep-fried bananas (goreng pisang) 145
  sesame & honey ice cream 174
  simplest coconut ice cream 146
  sweet almond pudding with poached apricots 204
  Vietnamese affogato 82
  yum cha mango pancakes 203
do chua (pickled carrot & daikon) 30
donburi, salmon & avocado 142
doria, prawn & avocado 101
dragon wing sauce 229
dragon wings 229
dressing 111
  bang-bang 58
  miso 74
  soy & sesame 78
dry-baked lamb chop curry with sweet potato 210
dry wonton noodles 122
duck
  buns 182
  pi-pa roast 49
  shoyu ramen 219
dumplings (siu mai) 231

E

egg custard, savoury 66
eggplant, miso-roasted 74
eggs, steeped 219
enriched béchamel 101

F

faster master (stock) 28
fillet steak with red miso butter 154
fish sauce ponzu 25
fish sauce roast chicken 126
five-spice salt 161
flan, leche 50
fresh herb & prawn salad 138
fresh sambal 36
fried mantou 129
furikake, chilli 33

G

garlic & shallot oil 21
garlic & soy sauce 195
Genghis Khan sauce 173
ginger & spring onion oil 81
ginger-fried pork 185
goreng pisang (Malaysian deep-fried bananas) 145
granita, lychee & coconut 116
gyudon (beef bowls) 125

H

hailam noodles 91
hot-buttered onigiri 62
hot chilli oil 24
hwachae 237

I

ice cream
  condensed milk 82
  sesame & honey 174
  simplest coconut 146

J

Japanese beef curry 169
Japanese tofu salad 111
Japanese triple-fried chicken (kara age) 121

K

kachumber 150
kara age (Japanese triple-fried chicken) 121
kimchi chigae (Korean pork & kimchi casserole) 108
kinilaw 189
Korean pork & kimchi casserole (kimchi chigae) 108
korokke, beef, with miso-mustard mayonnaise 170
kra-pow, chicken 158

L

lamb
    BBQ Genghis Khan 173
    dry-baked lamb chop curry with sweet potato 210
    northern Chinese roast 44
leche flan 50
lemongrass marinade 134
lemongrass pork chops, caramelised 134
Liaw family XO sauce 22
light teriyaki 32
lions' head meatballs 43
lions' heads 43
lychee & coconut granita 116

M

Malaysian barbecue fish 186
Malaysian deep-fried bananas (goreng pisang) 145
mantou, fried 129
marinades 44, 61, 91, 115, 126, 141, 166, 226
    base (for cheat's claypot) 107
    coconut & tamarind 234
    lemongrass 134
master stock 28
    fried chicken & five-spice salt 161
    poached chicken breast 81
mayonnaise, miso-mustard 170

mille-feuille with chilli ponzu 96
miso dressing 74
miso-mustard mayonnaise 170
miso-roasted eggplant 74
mushroom rice 162

N

Nagoya-style chicken wings 165
'no. 88' special fried rice 88
noodles
    chicken fat 141
    dry wonton 122
    duck shoyu ramen 219
    hailam 91
    sauce 122
    Singapore 73
northern Chinese roast lamb 44
nuoc cham sauce 134

O

ocean trout with garlic & soy 195
oil
    garlic & shallot 21
    ginger & spring onion 81
    hot chilli (ra-yu) 24
    onion 129
onigiri, hot-buttered 62
onion oil 129

P

pajeon, seafood 181
pak choy with oyster sauce 157
pan sushi 209
pancake batter 203
pancakes, mango yum cha 203
Penang achar 192
pi-pa roast duck 49
pickles
    asazuke 77

Penang achar 192
pickled carrot & daikon (do chua) 30
pineapple fried rice 200
ponzu, chilli 96
ponzu, fish sauce 25
pork
Balinese roast pork belly with fresh sambal 36
caramelised lemongrass pork chops 134
coconut & tamarind pork belly 234
ginger-fried 185
Korean pork & kimchi casserole (kimchi chigae) 108
lions' head meatballs 43
mille-feuille with chilli ponzu 96
pork & prawn wontons 214
salt & pepper pork belly 102
sang choy bao 130
siu mai 231
sweet & sour 199
winter pork & miso soup (tonjiru) 153
prawns
crystal prawns with celery 137
fresh herb & prawn salad 138
grilled with salty lime 196
pineapple fried rice 200
pork & prawn wontons 214
prawn & avocado doria 101
prawn paste 213
siu mai 231
sugarcane prawn rolls 213
XO prawns & snow peas 87
pumpkin & onion tempura, with curry salt 70

R
ra-yu (hot chilli oil) 24
red miso butter 154
rempah 192
rice
brown rice congee with crab 129
cheat's claypot 107
crab & lettuce fried 225

mushroom 162
'no. 88' special fried 88
pineapple fried 200
salmon & avocado donburi 142
sushi 209
two-to-one 40
rolls, sugarcane prawn 213

S
salad
bang-bang chicken 58
fresh herb & prawn 138
Japanese tofu 111
kachumber 150
spicy beansprout 112
spinach & sesame 78
salmon & avocado donburi 142
salt & pepper pork belly 102
salty lime 196
sambal 186
fresh 36
sang choy bao 130
sauce 157
bibimbap 178
chilli ponzu 96
cold roll (for sugarcane prawn rolls) 213
crying tiger 133
crystal prawns with celery, for 137
dipping 181
dragon wing 229
enriched béchamel 101
fish sauce ponzu 25
garlic & soy 195
Genghis Khan 173
hailam noodles, for 91
Liaw family XO 22
light teriyaki 32
noodle 122
nuoc cham 134
Singapore noodles, for 73

sweet & sour 199
umami 29
savoury egg custard 66
seafood
   brown rice congee with crab 129
   crab & lettuce fried rice 225
   crispy squid with chilli furikake 95
   crystal prawns with celery 137
   fresh herb & prawn salad 138
   grilled prawns with salty lime 196
   kinilaw 189
   Malaysian barbecue fish 186
   ocean trout with garlic & soy 195
   pajeon 181
   pan sushi 209
   prawn & avocado doria 101
   salmon & avocado donburi 142
   sugarcane prawn rolls 213
   XO prawns & snow peas 87
sesame & honey ice cream 174
short soup 65
simplest coconut ice cream 146
Singapore noodles 73
siu mai 231
soup
   short 65
   winter pork & miso (tonjiru) 153
soy & sesame dressing 78
soy broth 219
soy-dressed tofu 57
special fried rice, 'no. 88' 88
spicy beansprout salad 112
spinach & sesame salad 78
spring onion & ginger oil 81
squid, crispy, with chilli furikake 95
steak, fillet, with red miso butter 154
steeped eggs 219
stew, Vietnamese beef (bo kho) 222
stock
   faster master 28

white chicken 20
sugarcane prawn rolls 213
sushi, pan 209
sushi rice 209
sweet almond pudding with poached apricots 204
sweet & sour pork 199
sweet & sour sauce 199

T
tempura batter 70
tempura pumpkin & onion with curry salt 70
teriyaki chicken 92
teriyaki, light 32
tofu
   Japanese tofu salad 111
   soy-dressed 57
tonjiru (winter pork & miso) 153
trout, ocean, with garlic & soy 195
two-to-one rice 40

U
umami sauce 29

V
Vietnamese affogato 82
Vietnamese beef stew (bo kho) 222

W
white chicken stock 20
wonton noodles, dry 122
wontons, pork & prawn 214

X
XO beef & broccoli 61
XO prawns & snow peas 87
XO sauce 22

Y
yum cha mango pancakes 203

The idea that making good food is too hard, too expensive or takes too long is a fallacy that has been used to peddle a million unnecessary shortcuts, and it is one that deserves to be discarded forever. The act of cooking should be a joy and a gift.

If a recipe cooked from this book brings you a word of praise or a smile to the face of even just one of your loved ones, then you and I together will have achieved something truly wonderful.

I would love to hear from you so please visit me at:

www.twitter.com/adamliaw
www.adamliaw.com
www.facebook.com/AdamLiawFanPage

hachette
AUSTRALIA

Published in Australia and New Zealand in 2013
by Hachette Australia
(an imprint of Hachette Australia Pty Limited)
Level 17, 207 Kent Street, Sydney NSW 2000
www.hachette.com.au

10 9 8 7 6 5 4 3 2 1

National Library of Australia
Cataloguing-in-Publication data:

Liaw, Adam.

Asian after work / Adam Liaw

9780733630545 (pbk.)

Cooking, Asian.

641.595

Creative direction and design by Reuben Crossman
Photography by Steve Brown
Food styling by Lisa La Barbera
Food preparation by Nick Eade
Typeset in Charlet by House Industries, Haymaker by Trevor Baum
and Copernicus by Kris Sowersby
Printed in China by 1010 Printing International

With special thanks to the Sydney Fish Market and De Costi Seafoods.
Thanks also to EQ Village Markets at the Entertainment Quarter, Moore Park,
to Ceramicist Kris Coad (www.kriscoad.com) and Maria Altman.